# THE INFORMATION REVOLUTION IN ASIA

**Nina Hachigian**

**Lily Wu**

Prepared for the
National Intelligence Council

*National Defense Research Institute*

RAND

*Approved for public release; distribution unlimited*

The research described in this report was sponsored by the National Intelligence Council. The research was conducted in RAND's National Defense Research Institute, a federally funded research and development center supported by the Office of the Secretary of Defense, the Joint Staff, the unified commands, and the defense agencies under Contract DASW01-01-C-0004.

**Library of Congress Cataloging-in-Publication Data**

Hachigian, Nina.
    The information revolution in asia / Nina Hachigian, Lily Wu.
      p. cm.
    "MR-1719."
    ISBN 0-8330-3418-9 (pbk.)
      1. Information technology—Social aspects—Asia. 2. Information technology—
Asia. 3. Information society—Asia. I. Wu, Lily. II. Title.

HN655.2.I56H33 2003
303.48'33'095—dc21

                                           2003008743

Published 2003 by RAND
1700 Main Street, P.O. Box 2138, Santa Monica, CA 90407-2138
1200 South Hayes Street, Arlington, VA 22202-5050
201 North Craig Street, Suite 202, Pittsburgh, PA 15213-1516
RAND URL: http://www.rand.org/
To order RAND documents or to obtain additional information,
contact Distribution Services: Telephone: (310) 451-7002;
Fax: (310) 451-6915; Email: order@rand.org

# PREFACE

RAND is conducting a multiyear effort, sponsored by the National Intelligence Council, to explore the future of the information revolution throughout the world.[1] This multidisciplinary effort has a broad range of participants from both inside and outside RAND, with an overarching goal of mapping the likely future of the global information revolution over the next one to two decades.

This effort has included a series of international conferences on specific aspects of the information revolution, involving experts in various relevant areas. The proceedings of these conferences have been documented in the following RAND publications.

Richard O. Hundley, Robert H. Anderson, Tora K. Bikson, James A. Dewar, Jerrold D. Green, Martin C. Libicki, and C. Richard Neu, *The Global Course of the Information Revolution, Political, Economic, and Social Consequences: Proceedings of an International Conference*, RAND, CF-154-NIC, 2000.

Robert H. Anderson, Philip S. Antón, Steven K. Bankes, Tora K. Bikson, Jonathan A. Caulkins, Peter J. Denning, James A. Dewar, Richard O. Hundley, and C. Richard Neu, *The Global Course of the Information Revolution, Technological Trends: Proceedings of an International Conference*, RAND, CF-157-NIC, 2000.

---

[1]This effort is being carried out in support of the Information Revolution initiative of the DCI's Strategic Estimates Program.

Gregory F. Treverton and Lee Mizell, *The Future of the Information Revolution in Latin America: Proceedings of an International Conference*, RAND, CF-166-1-NIC, 2001.

Richard O. Hundley, Robert H. Anderson, Tora K. Bikson, Maarten Botterman, Jonathan A. K. Cave, C. Richard Neu, Michelle Norgate, and Renée Cordes, *The Future of the Information Revolution in Europe: Proceedings of an International Conference*, RAND, CF-172-NIC, 2001.

In addition to these international conferences, in-depth studies have been conducted on selected subjects. This publication reports the results of one of those studies—on the likely course of the information revolution in the Asia-Pacific region over the next five to ten years. Key questions addressed in this report include the extent to which the information revolution has taken hold in this region in general, the variations between individual countries, the prospects for further information-technology–related developments in the region, and the political implications of the information revolution for Asian governments.

Nina Hachigian is the director of RAND's Center for Asia Pacific Policy and a former member of the National Security Council staff; Lily Wu is a RAND consultant with 20 years of experience in the IT sector as an engineer, an entrepreneur, and investment banking analyst in Asia and the United States.

This research was sponsored by the National Intelligence Council and monitored by the National Intelligence Officer for Science and Technology. It was conducted by the Acquisition and Technology Policy Center of RAND's National Defense Research Institute (NDRI). NDRI is a federally funded research and development center sponsored by the Office of the Secretary of Defense, the Joint Staff, the defense agencies, and the unified commands.

# CONTENTS

# FIGURES

# TABLES

The information revolution is bringing about profound changes in political and economic life across the globe. RAND has embarked on a multiyear effort to chart trends in these changes out through the next ten to 20 years and around the world. The current volume investigates several aspects of the information revolution in the Asia-Pacific region, including the extent to which Asian nations produce or use information technology (IT), the political effect of such technology, and the future implications of IT for Asia.[2]

## THE INFORMATION REVOLUTION HAS HAD VARYING EFFECTS IN DIFFERENT ASIAN ECONOMIES

The question "what has been the effect of the information revolution on the economies in the Asia-Pacific region?" is best answered in two parts.[3] First, to what extent do Asian countries *use* information technology? Second, and equally important, to what extent do they *produce* IT hardware and software? Not surprisingly, the answer varies greatly on both counts. Figure S.1 shows (1) the major IT users and producers, (2) China and India (which are rapidly emerging as important IT users and producers), and (3) other economies that are

---

[2]To limit the scope of this report, and because we concentrated on drivers of IT use and production in Asia, we do not discuss in detail the "dark sides" of the information revolution—cyberwarfare, terrorists' exploitation of IT, loss of privacy, and governments' using IT to limit citizens' freedoms.

[3]By the "Asia-Pacific region" we mean all of Asia, including Australia, New Zealand, and most of the smaller islands of the Pacific Ocean. Throughout this report, we use "Asia" or "Asian" as a short form to refer to the entire Asia-Pacific region.

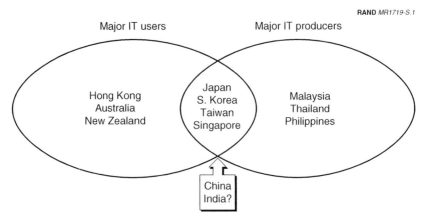

**RAND** *MR1719-S.1*

Figure S.1—IT Users and Producers in the Asia-Pacific Region

lagging well behind the rest of the region (and the world) in IT-related activities.

## SEVERAL ASIA-PACIFIC ECONOMIES ARE SIGNIFICANT USERS OR PRODUCERS OF INFORMATION TECHNOLOGY

Among the Asia-Pacific economies, Japan, South Korea, Singapore, and Taiwan are today both major users and producers of IT. Australia, Hong Kong, and New Zealand are large users but not producers, whereas Malaysia, the Philippines, and Thailand produce large quantities of technology products but are not big users. All of these economies are active participants in the information revolution.

## TODAY THE ASIA-PACIFIC REGION IS A MUCH MORE SIGNIFICANT GLOBAL IT PRODUCER THAN A CONSUMER

Japan, Singapore, Taiwan, South Korea, Malaysia, Thailand, and the Philippines are all major IT producers, with IT exports being a major fraction of the total economy in all of these nations except Japan. Indeed, the Asia-Pacific region is a much more significant global IT producer than a consumer.

Remarkably, *Asia accounts for more than 80 percent of the total world output of the following IT products:* desktop personal computers (PCs), notebook PCs, cathode ray tube (CRT) monitors, flat panel displays, modems, network interface cards, hard disk drives, computer mouse devices, keyboards, televisions, game boxes, mobile phones, personal digital assistants (PDAs), entry-level servers, hubs, and switches.

Asia is equally dominant in its output share of critical components and materials used in the IT industry. For the world's semiconductor industry, Asia produces over 70 percent of all bare silicon material, over 90 percent of epoxy resin for integrated circuit (IC) packaging, over 80 percent of memory semiconductors (dynamic random access memory (DRAM), static random access memory (SRAM), and flash memory), and over 75 percent of outsource manufactured semiconductors. Other critical IT parts made primarily in Asia include a wide range of passive components (resistors, diodes, and capacitors), connectors, sockets, switched power supplies, liquid crystal display (LCD) panels, printed circuit boards, and casings. Asia's share of global IT hardware output is not only large, it is still on a steep upward climb, as a growing number of ever higher-value parts and products get outsourced to the region for production.

In terms of IT use, in 2000, *Internet penetration in South Korea, Hong Kong, Japan, and Australia (in that order) exceeded even the U.S. level,* with Singapore, Taiwan, and New Zealand (in that order) not far behind. China represents one of the fastest growing markets, with the number of Internet users mushrooming from 22 million at the end of 2000 to over 60 million today. Asia is highly polarized, however; penetration of Internet use falls off by *one or two orders of magnitude* after the top ten countries. In contrast with the United States, most Internet use in Asia today is in the workplace, not the home.

Only in Japan and South Korea does home use exceed business use. Compared to other industrialized nations, use by businesses in Asia is not very sophisticated. Such functions as e-mail, supply chain management, and office automation dominate. There are several reasons for this, including a lack of successful business models, technical impediments such as network security, immature banking systems, a lack of government incentives, and the dominance of industries such as agriculture that do not demand sophisticated IT.

Home use, meanwhile, is limited in most Asian countries by insufficient resources, censorship (not widespread), and a lack of Internet content in the local language.

Asia's mobile phone use leads the world. China alone had over 200 million subscribers at the beginning of 2003, significantly more than any other country, including the United States. Although most of China's use is simple voice communication, Asia is also home to one of the most sophisticated mobile markets—Japan—where text messaging and other data services are popular. Taiwan and Hong Kong, each with over 80 percent mobile phone penetration, have among the highest use rates in the world.

## ASIAN NATIONS GENERALLY FOLLOW THE "JAPAN MODEL" IN THE EVOLUTION OF THEIR IT PRODUCTION ACTIVITIES

Asian IT producers have generally followed the "Japan Model" of progressively sophisticated production technology, beginning with labor-intensive, low-value manufacturing. The model, shown in Figure S.2, is a compromise of sorts between European top-down regulation and U.S. bottom-up entrepreneurialism.

Because they all follow the Japan Model, we can compare the industrial sophistication of the various Asian IT-producing economies according to their current positions in the model, as shown in Table S.1. South Korean and Taiwanese companies are thus among the more technologically advanced and diversified, after Japan, but they face challenges on the road to becoming global IT innovators. At the other end of the spectrum, most Southeast Asian IT producers appear to be stagnating at lower rungs on the production ladder. The reasons include their lack of indigenous IT companies and the rise of China (which we discuss below).

Across the Asia-Pacific region, extensive government assistance has played a significant role in fostering IT industries. That assistance has clearly been successful in establishing sizable IT manufacturing

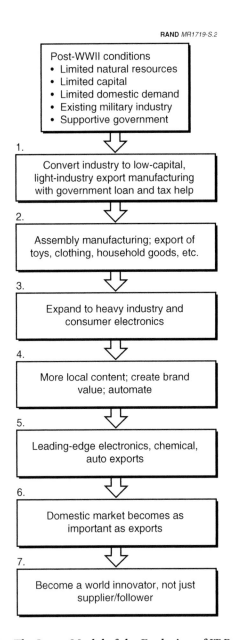

**Figure S.2—The Japan Model of the Evolution of IT Production**

Table S.1

**Sophistication of IT Producers in the Asia-Pacific Region**

| IT Producer | Stage | IT Ownership | Expertise |
|---|---|---|---|
| Japan | 7 | Domestic | Consumer electronics, advanced materials and components, IC design and manufacturing, computers |
| South Korea | 6 | Domestic | Consumer electronics, phones, peripherals, IC design and manufacturing |
| Taiwan | 5 | Domestic | PCs, peripherals, components, IC design and manufacturing, some communications equipment |
| Singapore | 4 | Domestic and foreign | Disk drives, PC peripherals assembly, some IC manufacturing |
| Malaysia | 3 | Foreign | Disk drives, PC peripherals assembly, cell phone assembly |
| Thailand | 2 | Foreign | Disk drives, disk drive component assembly |
| Philippines | 2 | Foreign | Peripherals assembly, some software, services |

industries where none existed previously, but we find that, over time, some government policies have limited competitiveness or led to corruption and inefficiency. For example, the Japanese government has directed banks to engage in "policy lending," i.e., lending to firms in certain sectors regardless of credit-worthiness. Companies in Korea, China, and Japan are actively adjusting to overcome the problems caused by such policies.

An impediment to a truly innovative Asian IT industry has been the predominance not only of government but also of banks and traditional industry as funding sources. All of these institutions are inherently conservative. Venture financing is virtually nonexistent, and most secondary stock markets formed in the boom years of the 1990s are small or languishing along with Nasdaq in the United States.

## CHINA AND INDIA ARE RAPIDLY EMERGING AS MAJOR IT USERS AND PRODUCERS

Clearly defined clusters of IT industry are already developing in China and, to a lesser extent, India, although IT output is far from being a major component of either country's economy. Both nations are following the early stages of the Japan Model in the evolution of their IT production activities, starting with low value-added production. Both governments, but especially China, have policies in place to encourage foreign companies to invest and produce locally, as well as incentives and allowances to foster home-grown IT companies. An assortment of lower-end hardware manufacturing dominates today in China, whereas back-office services and software outsourcing dominate in India.

China will almost surely advance, likely quickly, to later stages in IT industry development. The major driving force in China is the size and potential of its local market, and the almost endless availability of cheap labor, both of which attract foreign investment. In recent years, China has become the IT manufacturing base of choice, with Taiwanese and Hong Kong IT companies beginning to transfer their manufacturing operations there—a trend that is not only likely to continue but also accelerate—and has rapidly attracted a large knowledge base of increasingly advanced know-how.

India shares some of China's potential, especially in the software production sector, which has increased 50-fold over the past ten years to $7.6 billion in 2002. The environment in India, however, does not yet seem quite ripe to foster breakout development, despite an English language advantage. Software created in Bangalore or Hyderabad has negligible copyright protection, the domestic market is tiny, and manufacturing has not taken root. These factors, combined with a discouraging venture formation environment, have induced an outflow of engineers and other talent, mostly to the United States.

## WHAT DOES THE FUTURE HOLD FOR IT USE AND PRODUCTION IN ASIA?

We summarize the future outlook for IT use and production in the Asia-Pacific region as follows:

- Unique use solutions and local applications may be implemented, although few are likely to export well to U.S. or European markets.

- Tension between affordable service for consumers and reasonable returns for operators will probably continue and will be manifested in frequent government policy adjustments, volatile pricing, and a slowdown in the pace of IT innovation.

- Asia will continue to purchase state-of-the-art technologies, leap-frogging traditional infrastructure deficiencies.

- Although content control will continue to be a sporadic issue, it will give way to business and economic priorities over the long term, as governments increasingly realize that their countries' economic need for international connectivity is incompatible with strict content regulation.

- IT industries in Asia will flourish as manufacturing and services continue to be outsourced from other countries; China and India will attract the lion's share of this business.

- Innovative global market leadership will remain elusive for Asia's leaders in the short term.

- Governments will continue to exert influence as they engineer deregulation of telecommunications.

- IT industry financing will come from traditional venues for the foreseeable future, with leading-edge innovators continuing to flock to the United States.

## THE EFFECT OF THE INFORMATION REVOLUTION ON POLITICS AND GOVERNANCE IN THE ASIA-PACIFIC REGION ALSO VARIES WIDELY FROM NATION TO NATION

The information revolution is affecting politics and governance in the Asia-Pacific region largely through two dynamics:

- "Bottom-up" actions and initiatives of citizens, civil society, nongovernmental organizations (NGOs), and political parties using technology, ranging from organizing minor protests of government policies all the way to overthrowing sitting regimes.

- "Top-down" initiatives of governments that use technology to deliver information and services, generally termed electronic government or "e-government."

## INFORMATION TECHNOLOGY HAS HAD AN EFFECT ON POLITICS IN SOME ASIAN NATIONS, NOT IN OTHERS

All of the liberal democracies in Asia have virtually no restrictions on Internet access and online political use and content, whereas the authoritarian governments and illiberal democracies have a range of restrictions, as summarized in Table S.2.

A common assumption is that IT will have differing effects in regimes with differing political structures—common wisdom holds that IT will undermine closed regimes. Thus far, however, technology has not discriminated by regime type in its political effect. IT has had a significant effect on politics in some "one-party dominant" states and liberal democracies but not in others, as indicated in Table S.3. For example, IT has played a role in regime change in the democratic Philippines but also in Indonesia when it was a dictatorship. IT has

Table S.2

**Degree of Restrictions on Internet Political Use and Content, by Type of Government**

| **Severe Restrictions** on Online Political Content and Usage, Through Limits on Access | **Significant Restrictions** on Internet Access or Online Political Content and Usage, or Both | **Moderate Restrictions** on Political Content and Use; Promotion of Public Internet Access | **Negligible Restrictions** on Online Political Content and Use; Promotion of Internet Access |
|---|---|---|---|
| *Myanmar* <br> *North Korea* | *China* <br> *Vietnam* | *Singapore* | Australia <br> India <br> Indonesia <br> Japan <br> *Malaysia* <br> Philippines <br> South Korea <br> Thailand |

NOTE: One-party dominant states are shown in italics; liberal democracies are in normal type.

Table S.3

IT Influence on Politics, by Government Type

| Influence of IT on Politics | Type of Government | |
| --- | --- | --- |
| | One-Party Dominant States | Liberal Democracies |
| Visible influence | China Indonesia Malaysia | Philippines South Korea |
| No significant influence | Myanmar North Korea Singapore | Australia India Japan |

changed the political discourse in China, where the Communist Party rules alone, and in South Korea, where political parties compete, but not in authoritarian North Korea or in Australia, a liberal democracy. The reasons for this effect or lack thereof reflect a variety of conditions in each country including the degree of underlying flux in politics, IT penetration, and government control of the media.

## INFORMATION TECHNOLOGY IS RESHAPING THE WAY ASIA-PACIFIC GOVERNMENTS GOVERN, MORE IN SOME NATIONS THAN IN OTHERS

Several Asian governments routinely place within the top ten in the world in surveys of e-government activities; these include Australia, Singapore, Hong Kong, New Zealand, and Taiwan, with the first two consistently ranking among the most advanced e-government leaders in the world. Other countries are devoting significant amounts of time and resources to e-government but have not yet reached a level of global sophistication; those include Thailand, the Philippines, and Malaysia. Countries such as India and China have remarkable pockets of innovation in local government—with some Chinese officials at the provincial and local level enthusiastically embracing e-government—but they are in the early stages overall. Other nations, including North Korea, Myanmar, Vietnam, and Indonesia, have not developed notable e-government programs. E-government is changing some Asian governments—governments in Singapore and Hong Kong have become more efficient, and governments in South Korea have successfully fought corrupt practices using technology. The question for the future is whether these changes will fundamentally alter the relationship between governments and citizens.

## WHAT DOES THE FUTURE HOLD REGARDING THE EFFECT OF INFORMATION TECHNOLOGY ON POLITICS AND GOVERNANCE IN ASIA?

In the future, IT will no doubt play a large role in any political transitions that occur in wired countries in Asia. Moreover, NGOs will continue to exploit IT's potential to exert domestic and international pressure for policy change. Finally, e-government has the potential to usher in significant change in the relationship between government and citizens, but most such shifts will be gradual.

# ACKNOWLEDGMENTS

We would like to thank Richard Hundley for his intellectual guidance. We are also grateful to William Overholt and James Mulvenon for their thoughtful comments on early drafts. Joe Day and Sosi Maren deserve special mention for their encouragement.

# ACRONYMS

| | |
|---|---|
| ARPU | Average revenue per user |
| ASTRI | Applied Science and Technology Research Institute (Hong Kong) |
| CARD | Computer-Aided Administration of Registration Department (Andhra Pradesh, India) |
| CCP | Chinese Communist Party |
| CRM | Customer relationship management |
| CRT | Cathode ray tube |
| DRAM | Dynamic random access memory |
| EBITDA | Earnings before interest, taxes, depreciation, and amortization |
| ETRI | Electronics and Telecommunications Research Institute (South Korea) |
| GDP | Gross domestic product |
| GEM | Growth Enterprise Market |
| GSM | Global System for Mobile Communications |
| IC | Integrated circuit |
| ICT | Information and communications technology |

| | |
|---|---|
| IP | Internet protocol |
| IPO | Initial public offering |
| IRC | Internet Relay Chat |
| ISP | Internet service provider |
| IT | Information technology |
| ITRI | Industrial Technology Research Institute (Taiwan) |
| JETRO | Japan External Trade Organization |
| LCD | Liquid crystal display |
| LDP | Liberal Democratic Party (Japan) |
| MAI | Market for Alternative Investment (Thailand) |
| METI | Ministry of Economics, Trade, and Industry (Japan) |
| MSC | Multimedia Super Corridor (Malaysia) |
| NCM | New Capital Market (New Zealand) |
| NEC | National Elections Commission (South Korea) |
| NGO | Nongovernmental organization |
| NOIE | National Office for the Information Economy (Australia) |
| OEM/ODM | Original equipment design and manufacturing |
| OPEN | Online Procedures Enhancement for Civil Applications (South Korea) |
| PC | Personal computer |
| PCIJ | Philippine Center for Investigative Journalism |
| PDA | Personal digital assistant |
| R&D | Research and development |
| ROI | Return on Investment |

| | |
|---|---|
| SBA | Singapore Broadcast Authority |
| SLA | Service-level agreement |
| SMS | Short message service |
| SPDC | State Peace and Development Council |
| SRAM | Static random access memory |
| telco | Telecommunications company |
| VPN | Virtual private network |
| WHO | World Health Organization |
| WTO | World Trade Organization |

# Chapter One

# CURRENT STATUS OF THE INFORMATION REVOLUTION IN ASIA

*Lily Wu*

This chapter surveys the drivers that shape the current and future information technology (IT) landscape in Asia. IT's current status will be viewed from two major perspectives:

- Use and adoption of advanced information technology, and

- Production and creation of information technology.

To understand the factors driving and shaping the future of both IT use and production trends, we examine the history and development of models that exist today and key environmental factors, such as government policies and funding.

## ASIA'S IT USE, INFRASTRUCTURE, AND OUTPUT

Asia includes both the world's most advanced IT users and producers and also some of the least advanced (see Tables 1.1, 1.2, and 1.3).

### IT Penetration and Use

The most basic measure of a population's use of IT is its use of the Internet. Common measures used in the past, such as telephone or television use, do not capture the essence of today's information technology, which goes well beyond simply receiving locally broadcast information or holding one-on-one conversations. Internet use

### Table 1.1

### Internet Users per 1,000 People, 2000

| Advanced | No. of Users | Emerging | No. of Users | Laggards | No. of Users |
|---|---|---|---|---|---|
| South Korea | 402.7 | Brunei | 88.8 | Kazakhstan | 6.7 |
| Hong Kong | 382.5 | Thailand | 37.9 | Sri Lanka | 6.3 |
| Japan | 371.1 | Micronesia | 33.9 | India | 4.9 |
| Australia | 344.1 | Philippines | 26.5 | Uzbekistan | 4.8 |
| United States | 338.7 | Papua New Guinea | 26.3 | Solomon Islands | 4.5 |
| Singapore | 298.7 | China | 17.8 | Vietnam | 2.5 |
| Taiwan | 255.0 | Mongolia | 12.5 | Nepal | 2.2 |
| New Zealand | 216.7 | Kyrgyz | 10.5 | Bhutan | 1.9 |
| Malaysia | 159.0 | Marshall Islands | 9.6 | Turkmenistan | 1.2 |
| New Caledonia | 112.8 | Indonesia | 9.5 | Laos | 1.1 |

SOURCES: International Monetary Fund (2002); www.indianinfoonline.com; *Thai Economic Monitor* (2001); Taiwan economic data are from www.geoinvestor.com.

NOTE: Countries with one or less are Pakistan, Bangladesh, Cambodia, Tajikistan, and Myanmar.

measures the extent to which a country's people are proactively accessing, exchanging, and providing information on a global basis. By this measure, we find that Asia is home to markets with both the most IT use and the least in the world. Even in 2000, South Korea, Hong Kong, Japan, and Australia significantly exceeded the United States in the extent of Internet use, and Singapore has surpassed the United States since then. Japan, South Korea, Hong Kong, and Taiwan all had greater mobile phone use than the United States at the end of 2002 as well. However, Asia is highly polarized; Internet use falls off by *one or two orders of magnitude* after the top ten.

A corollary to IT penetration is the absolute size of IT markets. For example, Hong Kong society is one of the most "connected" and IT-fluent in the world with 383 users per 1,000 population. However, the total number of Internet users in 2000 was only 2.6 million, whereas China, a country with much lower IT penetration, had 22.5 million users. So although China is not an IT-fluent society as a whole, its influence on the global IT world is significantly greater. IT producers customize products and services for the China market, and global investment dollars are attracted to its sheer size. Table 1.2 shows the size of Asia's IT markets and identifies the major IT influencers. Underscoring just how influential and attractive China's

## Table 1.2
## Internet Market Size, 2000

| Large | Users (millions) | Year on Year Growth (%) | Medium | Users (millions) | Year on Year Growth (%) | Small | Users (thousands) | Year on Year Growth (%) |
|---|---|---|---|---|---|---|---|---|
| United States | 95.4 | 29 | Indonesia | 2.0 | 122 | Kazakhstan | 100.0 | 43 |
| Japan | 47.1 | 74 | Philippines | 2.0 | 52 | Kyrgyz | 51.6 | 50 |
| China | 22.5 | 153 | Singapore | 1.2 | 26 | Nepal | 50.0 | 43 |
| South Korea | 19.0 | 75 | New Zealand | 0.8 | 19 | Mongolia | 30.0 | 150 |
| Australia | 6.6 | 18 | Vietnam | 0.2 | 100 | Brunei | 30.0 | 20 |
| Taiwan | 5.7 | 28 | Papua New Guinea | 0.1 | 575 | New Caledonia | 24.0 | 100 |
| India | 5.0 | 178 | Pakistan | 0.1 | 67 | Myanmar | 7.0 | 1,300 |
| Malaysia | 3.7 | 48 | Sri Lanka | 0.1 | 87 | Laos | 6.0 | 200 |
| Hong Kong | 2.6 | 7 | Bangladesh | 0.1 | 100 | Cambodia | 6.0 | 50 |
| Thailand | 2.3 | 176 | Uzbekistan | 0.1 | 60 | Turkmenistan | 6.0 | 200 |

SOURCES: International Monetary Fund (2002); www.indianinfoonline.com; *Thai Economic Monitor* (2001); Taiwan economic data are from www.geoinvestor.com.

NOTE: Countries with 4,000 users or less are Micronesia, Tajikstan, the Solomon Islands, Bhutan, and the Marshall Islands.

Table 1.3

High-Technology Exports, 2000

|  | High-Tech Exports (U.S. $ millions) | High-Tech Exports as a % of Total Exports | High-Tech Exports as a % of GDP |
|---|---|---|---|
| United States | 367,919 | 34.0 | 3.7 |
| Japan | 135,564 | 28.0 | 2.8 |
| Singapore | 104,614 | 63.0 | 113.4 |
| Taiwan | 80,837 | 52.8 | 26.8 |
| Korea | 72,012 | 35.0 | 15.8 |
| Malaysia | 57,494 | 51.3 | 64.1 |
| Hong Kong | 56,111 | 23.0 | 34.5 |
| China | 53,349 | 19.0 | 4.9 |
| Thailand | 49,684 | 60.7 | 40.7 |
| Philippines | 24,692 | 59.0 | 33.0 |
| Australia | 22,965 | 15.0 | 5.9 |
| Indonesia | 9,563 | 16.0 | 6.2 |
| New Zealand | 1,597 | 10.0 | 3.2 |
| India | 1,408 | 2.2 | 0.3 |

SOURCES: International Monetary Fund (2002); www.indianinfoonline. com; *Thai Economic Monitor* (2001); Taiwan economic data are from www.geoinvestor.com.

IT market is, we note that its Internet user base exceeded 60 million in 2002, almost triple the level in 2000. Figure 1.1 shows China's remarkable growth.

The markets that "matter" are not only large, they also have high growth rates. Australia, Taiwan, and Hong Kong have already slowed to mature growth rates, as have Singapore and New Zealand among the medium-size markets.

It is also important to note that although the Asia IT market is relatively fast-growing, its absolute size is well below its 55 percent share of world population. In the first quarter of 2002, Asia accounted for 23.5 percent of personal computers (PCs) sold globally (Japan's share was 6.4 percent, and the rest of Asia's was 17.1 percent).[1] As we move higher up the technology ladder, Asia accounts for even smaller proportions of global IT consumption. In the fourth quarter of 2001, Asia accounted for 17.6 percent of servers sold globally; *and*

---

[1] International Data Corp. (2002f).

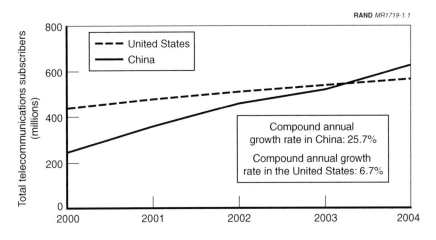

SOURCES: BDA Consultants, Gartner Dataquest, IDC, MII.

**Figure 1.1—Compound Annual Growth Rate in China and
the United States, 2000–2004**

the average price of a server sold in Asia was lower, at $10,375, than it was globally, at $11,025.[2]

Asia's mobile phone use is a more substantial market on the global scale. For example, China alone had over 200 million mobile subscribers at the end of 2002, making it the largest mobile market in the world, larger even than that of the United States.[3] However, 99 percent of China's mobile use is basic telephony (voice calls), which is the most basic IT application.[4] Asia is also home to some of the world's most sophisticated mobile markets, but they are smaller in comparison: Japan had 70.2 million mobile users in mid-2002, of which over 75 percent subscribe to data services and the Internet on their mobile phones.[5]

---

[2]International Data Corp. (2002d).

[3]*Asia Pacific Adds 104 Million Mobile Subscribers in 2002* (2003); Gupta (2003).

[4]J.P. Morgan (2001).

[5]"DoCoMo Director: Cell Phone Service Growth Too Slow" (2002).

## IT Producers

Finally, we should consider Asia's role in the global IT industry as a producer or manufacturer. From this perspective, Asia contributes well more than its proportionate share and is a dominant and critical global IT player. Remarkably, Asia accounts for more than 80 percent of the total world output of the following IT products: desktop PCs, notebook PCs, cathode ray tube (CRT) monitors, flat panel displays, modems, network interface cards, modems, hard disk drives, computer mouse devices, keyboards, televisions, game boxes, mobile phones, personal digital assistants (PDAs), entry-level servers, hubs, and switches.[6]

Asia is equally dominant in its output share of critical components and materials used in the IT industry. For the world's semiconductor industry, Asia produces over 70 percent of all bare silicon material, over 90 percent of epoxy resin for integrated circuit (IC) packaging, over 80 percent of memory semiconductors (dynamic access random memory (DRAM), static random access memory (SRAM), and flash memory), and over 75 percent of outsource manufactured semiconductors. Other critical IT parts made primarily in Asia include a wide range of passive components (resistors, diodes, and capacitors), connectors, sockets, switched power supplies, liquid crystal display (LCD) panels, printed circuit boards, and casings. Asia's share of global IT hardware output is not only large, it is still on a steep upward climb, as a growing number of ever-higher-value parts and products get outsourced to the region for production. Applied Materials, the leading world maker of semiconductor manufacturing equipment, notes that in the first quarter of 2002, 71 percent of its equipment was sold to Asia, compared to 41 percent in 1996.[7] This is a leading indicator that Asia's semiconductor output will as much as double in the years to come.

Table 1.3 provides insight into Asia's leading IT producers in absolute terms and also in terms of how critical IT exports are to eco-

---

[6]Taiwan Market Intelligence Center press releases.

[7]Applied Materials annual financial reports, filed with the U.S. Securities Exchange Commission (2001, 2002).

nomic performance.[8] In particular, IT exports are a top component of the economy in Singapore, Taiwan, Malaysia, Thailand, and the Philippines.

## Major IT Players

We categorize Asia's key IT players in Figure 1.2 in major groupings, which will be referred to in the remainder of this chapter. These groupings are the major IT users, major IT producers, major IT users *and* producers, and the outliers. China is of special note (and India,

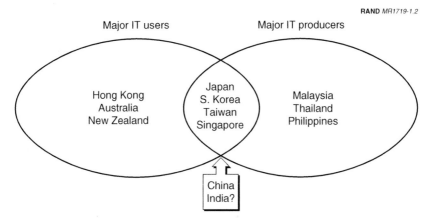

Not major IT users or producers: Indonesia, Pakistan, Cambodia, Laos, Central Asia, and others

**Figure 1.2—IT Users and Producers**

---

[8]To avoid misinterpreting the data, the following two points should be noted: (1) A large proportion of Hong Kong's IT exports is actually produced in China by Taiwan-owned companies. Taiwanese companies typically hold their Chinese manufacturing subsidiaries under Hong Kong-based overseas entities to circumvent Taiwanese government restrictions on direct investment in China or ownership of China-based entities. (2) In Singapore and Malaysia's data, exports are reported in total value, including the value of parts that were imported to, but not produced in, Singapore or Malaysia. For example, a $75 hard-disk drive is exported, but local value added may have been only $35, because $40 in unassembled components was imported. That explains the unusually high IT export value as a percentage of GDP.

to a lesser extent), since it is a rapidly emerging major IT user and producer. We note below that within each grouping, the individual IT development histories, key driving factors, and key challenges and limiters are very similar.

## COMMERCIAL IT USE

Without a doubt, the Internet has penetrated all segments of virtually every country in the world, but the degrees vary considerably in Asia.

### Business Dominates Asia's Internet Access

In advanced IT use markets with high Internet user penetration, such as the United States, Japan, and Korea, the primary point of access is the home or other points of private use, such as PC arcades, Internet cafes, or personal mobile devices. This is a significant indication that IT use in advanced markets has become integrated into the users' way of life and daily living, and personal investment has been made in purchasing or renting an Internet access device. Advanced IT use markets correlate well with both wealth and early literacy. Another reason for high rates of home or private access to IT in these markets is use by children and young adults, who are IT literate at an early age. The key IT applications that account for the greatest amount of time spent on home or private Internet access include communication (e-mail, instant messaging), entertainment (gaming, music, film, photo-sharing), e-commerce (shopping, gambling), and education (news, information-gathering).

The majority of Asia, however, lacks either the wealth or the IT literacy required for personal IT or Internet usage, or both, which leaves access limited to only those with a computer at work in either a private company or a government office. Schools in virtually all countries are also access points for IT but mainly in higher education institutions and with tens or hundreds of users per machine. With such limited access, primarily through businesses, it is not surprising that Internet use falls off by one or two orders of magnitude after only a handful of advanced IT use countries (see Table 1.1). It is estimated that although the home or other private access point accounts for approximately 50 percent of primary Internet use in the advanced markets of the United States, Japan, and Korea, the home accounts for less than 10 percent of Internet use access in Thailand and the Philippines and less than 5 percent in Indonesia. China and Vietnam are notable for their high proportions (over one-third) of primary Internet access through schools, reflecting a young IT user population and government policies that support IT infrastructure in universities.

## Applications Not Yet Sophisticated

Although businesses are the leading mode of access to the Internet for Asia, uses are not highly sophisticated. Aside from basic e-mail and office automation, the primary use is supply chain management, resulting from Asia's significant export manufacturing industry. On-line supply chain transactions were the largest category of Internet commerce in Asia, accounting for 27.3 percent of the total $7.25 billion e-commerce market in 2000.[9]

Another customer-oriented import/export Internet application that Asia has taken up readily is customer relationship management (CRM) software. CRM consists of multimillion-dollar software and systems enterprise applications for identifying, tracking, fulfilling, and servicing a business' customer requests and communications. CRM systems also tie into a company's back office for invoicing, billing, and credit. In 2001, the global CRM market was $16.35 billion; Japan accounted for $2.9 billion or 17.7 percent, with the rest of Asia totaling $1.8 billion, or 11 percent. Aside from Japan, leading adopter countries of note are Australia, South Korea, and Singapore.[10] From a global economic perspective, Japan accounted for 15.4 percent of world gross domestic product (GDP) in 2000, and Asia, minus Japan, accounted for 8.4 percent of world GDP.[11]

Aside from the basic use of e-mail and supply and customer management, only an estimated 15 percent of all networked businesses had Internet protocol-based (IP-based) virtual private networks (VPNs) in 2000.[12] Having an IP VPN is the minimum requirement to

---

[9]International Data Corp. (2000).

[10]International Data Corp. (2002a, 2002b, 2002e).

[11]World Bank (2001).

[12]International Data Corp. (2001).

move into higher value-added services or applications such as mobile workforce deployment with real-time connectivity, remote dial-up access, firewall and authentication services needed to complete secure financial transactions, IP telephony, unified messaging, application software outsourcing, web or content hosting, and collocation. Indeed, only a further 9 percent of networked companies that did not have an IP VPN said they had plans to implement one in the coming year. Considering the global IT market slowdown, which worsened through 2000 and 2001, it is safe to assume that only a fraction of that 9 percent has actually since implemented one.[13]

## Barriers to Use

Businesses are leading the initial Internet and IT charge in Asia, and the clear driver is the need to be tied into the global economy and trade. Exports are a key component of most Asian businesses, and the Internet is a "must" for maintaining contact with overseas customers. Indeed, most Asian businesses of any size will have a web presence and a basic network for e-mail. However, beyond that, we do find numerous inhibitors to greater use of advanced applications aside from simply e-mail and supply and customer management.

**No Models to Follow.** The most stubborn inhibitor to greater IT or Internet use by businesses is the current lack of good profitable business models. However, there are examples of solidly run businesses that have faltered on greater use of or reliance on IT. We will consider three high profile publicly listed companies: Global Sources (Nasdaq: GSOL), Tom.com (HK GEM: 8001), and NTT (TSE: 9432). We will then consider the potential for success and the reasons why Asian countries have not achieved it.

*Discouraging Examples.* Global Sources is an "old economy" business established in 1971 as a media company, publishing magazines for global buyers needing to source products from Asia in volume. By 1995, Global Sources was far and away the best-known and largest provider of business-to-business trade information from Asia. It catalogued over 100,000 suppliers in Asia into 14 industry sectors for

---

[13]International Data Corp. (2001).

over 300,000 active buyers globally and processed millions of requests for information annually.[14]   One imagines that the Internet would be ideal for a company like Global Sources.   Indeed, in 1995, it launched an online business division, which management envisioned would eventually replace all of its traditional print and CD-ROM-based businesses.   Since 1995, although global trade and sourcing from Asia reach new peak levels every year, Global Sources' revenue has stagnated and profitability has fallen (see Table 1.4).

A key issue cited by Global Sources management in interviews is that although people expect to pay for magazine subscriptions, web content is perceived to be either free or very cheap.   Online advertising also does not command as high a price as print advertising, even though the viewership and content is the same in either medium.

### Table 1.4

### Global Sources, Ltd., Financial Summary, FY97 and FY01 (U.S. $ millions)

| Item | 1997 | 2001 | Comments |
|---|---|---|---|
| Online market services | 5.1 | 55.5 | Web subscriber fees, creating and hosting sites, banner ads |
| Media services | 94.8 | 35.0 | Magazine subscription fees, traditional advertising |
| Total revenue | 99.9 | 90.5 | No revenue growth over the last four years |
| Circulation cost | 20.1 | 11.8 | Web-based circulation is much cheaper than printing magazines |
| General administrative costs | 39.5 | 33.7 | Managing a website is cheaper overall than traditional media |
| Sales cost | 28.6 | 32.0 | Cost to get a customer to pay for a web subscription is greater |
| Online services development | 1.4 | 8.4 | Cost to develop value-added web businesses such as hosting |
| Total costs | 89.6 | 85.9 | |
| Operating profit | 10.3 | 4.6 | |
| Operating margin, % | 10.3 | 5.1 | Profitability cut in half, despite booming Asia trade and sourcing |

SOURCES: Global Sources annual financial reports, filed with the U.S. Securities Exchange Commission.

---

[14]Global Sources annual financial reports, filed with the U.S. Securities Exchange Commission.

Commercial use of the web has not only reduced value and profitability for Global Sources; it will inevitably put the company out of business if some new business model is not devised.

Tom.com is a "new economy" business established in 1998 by one of Hong Kong's leading tycoons, Li Ka-Shing, who owns controlling interest in Hong Kong Electric Company, Hutchison Whampoa (a leading trading and services company), in Cheung Kong (Hong Kong's largest property company), and in numerous others. Tom.com was established as a content and e-commerce portal and has continually been one of the ten most visited sites in Asia since its inception. In 2000, it was the first company to list on Hong Kong's new Nasdaq-like Growth Enterprise Market (GEM).[15] Tom.com appears to be a home-grown Asia IT commercial success story. That assessment is correct, but not for reasons having anything to do with IT.

Tom.com has turned out to be an Asia media commercial success story. Although Tom.com was envisioned to derive all of its earnings from IT use and the Internet, it became clear early in 2000 that this was not possible, in part because of problems similar to those afflicting Global Sources. People were not willing to pay for anything on the web. In late 2000, a new management team was brought in, who are maintaining the website for its future "possibilities" but who aggressively pursue traditional media sources for advertising, publishing, and event revenue (see Table 1.5).

Even the mobile phone success stories in Japan, Korea, and China have been bittersweet commercially. Mobile revenue and profits have soared, but at the expense of traditional wire line revenues, and often at lower margins, leaving the telecommunications companies (telcos) less profitable overall. NTT Docomo is a success story and pioneer in the mobile phone industry. It serves 56 percent of the mobile phone users in Japan, and over 75 percent of its customers use advanced mobile services such as web browsing, m-commerce, instant messaging, gaming, music downloads, and e-mail. Its revenue and profitability have grown steadily over the last five years. But the story does not end there.

---

[15]"Information on Listed Companies."

Table 1.5

Tom.com Financial Summary, F2Q01 and F1Q02
(H.K. $ millions)

| Item | 2Q01 | 1Q02 | Comments |
|------|------|------|----------|
| On-line revenue | 32.0 | 38.0 | Web-based advertising and e-commerce revenue |
| Off-line revenue | 113.0 | 227.0 | Magazines, books, billboards, unipoles, music, and promotions |
| Total revenue | 145.0 | 265.0 | 83 percent increase in revenue over last four quarters driven by traditional media businesses |
| Operating cost | 223.0 | 339.9 | |
| Operating profit | (78.0) | (74.9) | |

SOURCES: Tom.com quarterly financial reports, filed with the Hong Kong Growth Enterprise Market Securities and Futures Commission.

NTT Docomo is the mobile subsidiary of NTT, Japan's largest telecom company. NTT's other subsidiaries, NTT East and NTT West (local telephone operating companies) and NTT Communications (long distance company) have been in equally steady decline. Overall, NTT Group's revenue growth has not been impressive, and its profitability has stagnated (Table 1.6). Even NTT Docomo's earnings may have peaked as the Japan mobile market becomes saturated. A worrying indicator is that NTT Docomo's average revenue per user (ARPU) is in steady decline; Internet and data use have increased, but at the expense of voice calls (see Table 1.6). Thus far, ARPU decline has been offset by a growing user base, but management expects the user base to level off soon as mobile penetration exceeds 60 percent, and competition from emerging service providers J-Phone and KDDi intensifies. In contrast, ARPU for wireline customers has been stable and growing for over 40 years; the wireless business is inherently more competitive, and rapid technology advances and sustained interest for specific value-added services have been elusive.[16]

---

[16]For example, at the second-largest telecommunications company in the United States, SBC, wire-line revenue was down $332 million year on year in 1Q02, whereas mobile was up only $95 million. In addition, the mobile EBITDA (earnings before interest, taxes, depreciation, and amortization) margin is 31.2 percent, well below the wire-line EBITDA margin of 41.6 percent. Even Verizon, the leading U.S. wireless company, was able to grow mobile revenue by only $328 million year on year in 1Q02, compared to a decline of $446 million in wire-line.

**Table 1.6**

**NTT Consolidated Financial Summary, FY00 to FY03**

| | March 00 | March 01 | March 02 | Forecast March 03 | Comments |
|---|---|---|---|---|---|
| **NTT Group (yen, billions)** | | | | | |
| Revenue | 10,421.1 | 11,414.2 | 11,681.6 | 11,969.0 | |
| Operating profit | 980.3 | 898.3 | 947.3 | | |
| Revenue change year on year, % | | 9.5 | 2.3 | 2.5 | Growth rate is unimpressive |
| Operating profit margin, % | 9.4 | 7.9 | 8.1 | | Profitability has not improved |
| **NTT Docomo (yen)** | | | | | |
| Average revenue/ user/month | | 8,980 | 8,480 | 8,030 | Revenue per mobile user dropping |
| i-Mode | | 880 | 1,540 | 1,663 | i-Mode revenue per user has doubled |
| Voice | | 8,100 | 6,940 | 6,367 | Voice call revenue keeps falling |

SOURCES: NNT Corp. and NTT Docomo annual financial statements filed with the Tokyo Stock Exchange.

*Problems in Translating Success Stories Elsewhere.* Without a doubt, successful, profitable, and sustainable businesses are possible in the new IT economy. Examples are most notable in the United States, including well-known names such as Ebay, Yahoo!, and Amazon. Less well known, but equally successful and profitable, are others such as Expedia, a leading online travel booking service; PayPal, a centralized bill payment and banking service company for individuals and small businesses; and WebEx, an online conference service provider that allows business partners to share slides and talk (meet) together real-time over the Internet. WebEx has been especially popular in the last year as people are cost-conscious and less inclined to travel. A snapshot of these companies is provided in Table 1.7.[17]

For various reasons, such business models have not taken hold yet in Asia, but certainly not for lack of trying. For example, Yahoo! is one

---

[17]There are numerous other IT business successes, including IT infrastructure and software suppliers such as Cisco, Sun Microsystems, and i2 Technologies. Traditional companies such as Dell Computers have also steadily increased their Internet sales proportion.

Table 1.7

**Successful New-Economy IT Companies (revenue ending 2Q02, in U.S. $)**

|  | Ebay | Yahoo! | Expedia | Amazon | PayPal | WebEx |
|---|---|---|---|---|---|---|
| Revenue ($ millions) | 266.3 | 225.8 | 145.0 | 806.0 | 53.8 | 33.2 |
| Revenue increase over last year, % | +47 | +24 | +85 | +21 | +173 | +80 |
| Net profit ($ millions) | 54.3 | 21.4 | 29.2 | (4.0) | 0.5 | 2.4 |
| Market capitalization ($ billions) | 15.6 | 8.1 | 2.7 | 5.3 | 1.2 | 0.6 |
| Business focus | Online auction | Internet portal | Online travel bookings | Online retailer | Online bill payment | Web-based conferences |

SOURCES: Financial press releases for the second quarter of 2002, from investor relations section of www.ebay.com, www.yahoo.com, www.expedia.com, www.amazon.com, www.paypal.com, and www.webex.com.

of the original and most basic IT business models: a portal. Internet portals have sprung up throughout Asia, none of which has been able to gain mass or profitability. Tom.com, for example, was meant to be a Yahoo! but quickly reverted to traditional media to grow (although it is still not profitable). China's Sohu.com and Sina.com have yet to turn a profit, and their quarterly revenues have stagnated at the $6 million and $7 million levels, respectively (and even these levels were achieved in the June quarter only because of the World Cup). Yahoo! derives all of its sizable $225.8 million quarterly revenue from the Internet: 60 percent from marketing services such as ads, e-mail drives, and site links; 33 percent from fees for listings and directories; and 7 percent from e-commerce transaction fees.[18] At this scale of revenue, Yahoo! is a sustainable business; it is profitable, can reinvest for growth, and can afford high-quality content.

For many reasons, Asia does not have IT businesses similar to those in Table 1.7. One reason is the geographically and linguistically fractured nature of Asia; the U.S. market, in contrast, constitutes a sizable single market. Asia has also arguably not yet achieved the minimum Internet user penetration and per capita wealth needed to

---

[18]Yahoo! first-quarter 2002 financial report (10-K form), filed with the U.S. Securities Exchange Commission.

make its IT businesses a success. However, the more stubborn underlying reason has to do with Asia's approach to traditional media itself. Until very recently, the large majority of all media companies in Asia were either directly state-owned, or quasi state-owned and were sold to the public at highly subsidized rates as a public service. Even the few privately owned media companies tended to be subsidized by tycoons or conglomerates who fancied being newspaper owners. Advertising rates in Asian media are a fraction of those in the United States. The tradition of paying fair market value for media and respecting the copyrights of their content is weak, to say the least. The initial perception of the Internet as free or low cost did not help, accounting for the inability of Global Sources to get its subscribers to pay similar rates for content online that was identical to what they paid for in magazines or on CDs. We also know from anecdotal evidence that although piracy of music and film is a global problem, it seems much worse in Asia than in the United States or Europe. And even when legitimate payment is made, an average Asia movie ticket or local artists' music costs much less than in the United States (Japan being the major exception). The media industry, in general, is in transition in Asia, and IT businesses face unique challenges finding solid footing in the meantime.

The other businesses highlighted in Table 1.7 are primarily e-tailing in nature (electronic retailing). Although e-tailing has grown in Asia, its scale remains small and fragmented, and it is challenged by the ubiquitous low-cost nature of traditional retailing. For example, Americans are increasingly booking their own travel online through Expedia or Travelocity; Expedia's second quarter 2002 revenue of $145 million represents fees on $1.33 billion in travel bookings.[19] In Taipei, Hong Kong, or Seoul, there is a cheap, helpful travel agent at virtually every other street corner, who will deliver your tickets to your door with no extra charge. The most notable success in retail Internet use thus far in Asia has been gaming and gambling. Some of it is illegal, so aggregated statistics are not readily available, but it is sizable and profitable enough for Hong Kong's government to crack

---

[19]Expedia first-quarter 2002 financial report (10-K form), filed with the U.S. Securities Exchange Commission.

down and view it as a major threat to its public finances.[20]  WebEx-type businesses may do well in Asia, but establishing them will take time as businesses upgrade their IT infrastructure.

The bottom line is that every business cost must have a clear return or ultimate financial benefit.  Basic networking and a web presence is a must for Asian businesses to communicate internally and with customers, but beyond that, there is no proven body of cases of solid financial return for greater IT investment.  As long as reasonable return on investment remains elusive, many in the private sector will remain on the sidelines of advanced IT use.

**Network Security and Reliability Barriers.**  Some technology and financial infrastructure barriers also remain in the way of greater or more sophisticated business and commercial use of IT.  These issues will be increasingly addressed by the rapid pace of technology advances.  In the March 2001 IDC survey mentioned above, where only 15 percent of Asia's networked companies had IP VPNs, the negative respondents were polled for their reasons for not implementing an IP VPN.  The top five reasons were (three reasons tied for second place):[21]

1.  Lack of network security

2.  Poor or no monitoring and management services

3.  High cost

4.  No SLA (service-level agreements)

5.  Limited geographic availability.

Although there are many advantages to having a web-based, remotely accessible network, corporate IT managers, and even governments, are clearly concerned that it makes them more vulnerable to cyber-crime and hacking.  This is primarily a technology issue,

---

[20]BBC News (2002).  A major source of the Hong Kong government's revenue is taxes paid by the local gambling monopoly, Jockey Club.

[21]International Data Corp. (2001).

where much private and public sector effort is being expended to find robust and easy-to-implement solutions. Asian businesses face the same IT security challenges, using the same network infrastructure as any other global business, but the high incidence of local disregard for copyright and intellectual property protection in traditional businesses probably makes an Asian business leader more sensitive to this concern than his or her western counterpart.

Inability to monitor and manage a network effectively is a related concern to security and to the SLA issue of network reliability. Remotely managed or globally distributed IP VPN networks are prone to transmission congestion, bottlenecks, or system crashes. Already, significant advances even in the last year have been made to improving the quality and reliability of IP networks. Reliability, accountability, and geographic reach of network providers (SLAs) are ongoing areas of improvement in this steadily maturing business.

**Financial Infrastructure Barriers.** The financial infrastructure issue is related to e-commerce or e-tailing; how does an Asian Internet user complete a transaction online? Credit cards are overwhelmingly the payment method of choice. Not surprisingly, countries with high rates of online transaction completion have mature banking systems and widespread use of credit. Markets where over 60 percent of e-commerce transactions are actually completed online are Japan, Korea, Australia, New Zealand, Hong Kong, Singapore, and Taiwan.[22]

Countries where only 8 to 14 percent of e-commerce transactions are completed online include Malaysia, China, Thailand, the Philippines, Indonesia, India, and Vietnam.[23] In these cases, e-commerce represents buying decisions made online but actually completed offline in some other physical way. Lack of a credit card system is an inhibitor to e-commerce in these countries, but the hurdle is one that can be overcome and has been in some countries. Alternative, and equally effective, payment systems being adopted include debit cards, prepaid cards, and direct account transfers (commonly used for stock transactions). A more cumbersome payment method popular in China is fund transfers made through post offices.

---

[22]International Data Corp. (2000).

[23]International Data Corp. (2000).

## IT INDUSTRIES AND DEVELOPMENT MODELS BY COUNTRY

In Asia, the driving forces to high IT use and high IT production are surprisingly distinct from each other. Being a major user does not necessarily lead to major production, nor vice versa. Of the countries that are both major IT users and producers, only Japan and Korea have gained some synergistic advantages between the two, and even that is only very recently, and with limited degrees of success. We will therefore consider the development models of the users and producers separately.

### Major Users

**Promoting Factors.** In Table 1.1, the extent of IT use is listed by geographic market. The leading seven are on par with the United States, and well ahead of the rest of the continent. High IT penetration in each of these markets came about from some combination of the following factors:

1. Wealth (affordability of services and devices),

2. Business imperative (office automation, supply chain, and e-mail),

3. Relative quality of content and applications (compared to existing traditional media/communications),

4. Availability of local language content and applications,

5. Government policies, and

6. Existing infrastructure.

*Korean Phoenix.* The specific combination of driving factors that prevail in any given country can be quite unusual. For example, Korea's high standard of living made it an early but not aggressive IT adopter in the 1990s. Starting in 1997, its Internet and mobile phone penetration soared to put it first in the world; the driving factors, surprisingly, were factors 3, 4, and 5. Korea was one of the hardest hit in Asia's currency crisis in 1997—it defaulted on sovereign debt and was bailed out with a plan from the International Monetary Fund. Unprecedented layoffs, bankruptcies, and corporate consolidations followed.  In a culture not known for its entrepreneurialism, this led to a rash of startup companies founded by laid-off, though highly qualified, professionals.  Many focused on creating new IT content, applications, and services for the local market.  Additionally, *PC Pangs*—arcades stocked with PCs for hourly use—sprang up everywhere.  People of all ages with plenty of free time, including businessmen, crowded into the *PC Pangs* primarily for online trading and gaming.  The hourly rate is a low W1,400–W2,000 (about $1).  Access to IT was therefore universally affordable through the *PC Pangs*, with no upfront cost or infrastructure required, and at a time when a plethora of applications tailored to the local market in Korean became available.  The wide availability of broadband access fueled this trend.  Also, to sweeten the IT use deal, government-enforced competition drove mobile carriers to offer subsidies of over 50 percent on the price of a mobile handset, which rocketed the mobile user base from three million at the end of 1996, to 21 million in 1999, a period when consumer activity was weak overall because of the currency crisis.  Korea's mobile user base today exceeds 33 million (68 percent penetration, compared to phone line penetration of 45 percent).[24]

*Chinese Leapfrog.*  Another interesting market is China.  Aggressively using technology advances, China is in the process of making a giant jump from the bottom of Asia's infrastructure heap to likely becoming one of the most advanced in the coming years.  Although actual PC, mobile phone, and Internet penetration rates are still low, China's growth rates in these areas are among the highest in the world.  Traditional phone line penetration in China has stagnated around nine lines per 100 people, and mobile phone use is 16 per 100 people and growing.[25]  The problem is that an urban phone line application takes months to fill and requires a large deposit and a relatively permanent home address (a rural phone application can take years).  On the other hand, a mobile phone can be bought at any time with immediate service using GSM (Global System for Mobile Applications) prepaid cards.  Although few homes are wired for cable TV, many urban families receive it anyway using satellite dishes.  PC access is

---

[24]*Asia Pacific Adds 104 Million Mobile Subscribers in 2002* (2003); Gupta (2003); See also Choi et al. (2000).

[25]*Asia Pacific Adds 104 Million Mobile Subscribers in 2002* (2003); Gupta (2003); J.P. Morgan (2001).

cheaply available in schools and at Internet cafes (2,400 in Beijing alone), and going online will soon be possible wirelessly.  Aside from factor 3 (quality of content), factors 2 (business imperative) and 4 (local language content) are also significantly at play in China.  China's rapid advances in IT use are driven by these underlying factors but, equally important, are occurring in the context of an encouraging government that views IT prowess as a key to modernization and economic advancement.

The remaining high-IT-use markets rely on factors 1 (wealth) and 6 (existing infrastructure).  Australia, New Zealand, Hong Kong, and Singapore are wealthy markets, and all homes and offices are wired anyway.  Custom localized applications have developed in all four but were not requisites, since English comprehension is widespread.

**Inhibitors and Lurking Concerns.**  There is no distinct set of factors inhibiting IT use in Asia—the countries that lag are faced with the negative version of the driving factors.  For example:

1. Insufficient wealth—population cannot afford even a basic phone or PC use fee,

2. Agrarian, natural resources, or developing economies with no compelling need for business IT,

3. Traditional media meet current needs or have not yet saturated the market,

4. Lack of either English proficiency or local language applications and content, and

5. Government has no IT initiative, or heavily taxes electronics sales, or censors media content.

Some emerging IT use markets, such as Thailand and Malaysia, are actively addressing the issues listed above although, ultimately, the key is the overall level of economic development.  The compelling hurdles are affordability and content/application quality.  Infrastructure is not an issue, since technology is available to install on any existing level of platform.  Even in the United States, for example, over 90 percent of homes have access to high-speed Internet service via phone lines, cable TV, or satellite, but only 7 percent subscribe.  The key issue is factor 3 listed above:  the content and applications avail-

able are not considered differentiated enough to be worth the sub-
scription fees.[26]

Other countries such as China, India, and Vietnam are becoming
highly bifurcated IT markets. All three countries have urban centers
that are highly IT penetrated, whereas their rural and remote areas
remain untouched. Shanghai's mobile phone penetration is 46 percent of households, compared to 16 percent for the country.[27] This
divide is likely to widen before narrowing, with driving factors apply-
ing in cities and inhibiting factors prevailing in rural areas.

One lurking concern that faces all Asian countries is the possibility of
an IT backlash or slowdown in the future. Natural business forces
may lead to a slowdown because some of the key drivers of consumer
IT use in Asia are the same factors that inhibit greater IT use in businesses. For example, excessive competition, which makes it difficult
for businesses to sustain profits from IT, is providing consumers with
more extensive, better quality, and cheaper communications access
than ever before, and richer, cheaper, and more diverse content and
applications. Table 1.8 summarizes these factors.

Already in some markets, Internet service providers (ISPs) and hosting companies have gone out of business; portals such as Tom.com
and Pacific Century Cyberworks have reverted to traditional media;
mobile companies such as SK Telecom have intentionally delayed
launching new services such as 3G; NTT has pushed out its broadband launch; etc. Another stark example of this concern is found in
Korea; starting in 1996, Korea's three mobile carriers competed aggressively for new mobile subscribers by heavily subsidizing handset
cost. By the end of 1998, accumulated subsidy payments amounted
to $1.9 billion, and the carriers' debt to capital ratio reached as high
as 1,108 percent. Financial disaster was avoided as foreign investors
piled into Korea in 1999 (when global stock markets were still riding
high and cash was plentiful).[28] The danger is that if the IT business
remains fundamentally unprofitable, or only marginally profitable,

---

[26]Federal Communications Commission (2002).

[27]J.P. Morgan (2001).

[28]Choi et al. (2000).

Table 1.8

Business IT Inhibitors Are Consumer IT Drivers

| New Economy Characteristic | Effect on Businesses | Effect on Consumers |
|---|---|---|
| More competitors than in traditional media and communications sectors | **Negative:** Competition means lower fees and higher cost to attract customers | **Positive:** More suppliers to choose from and better quality of service |
| New IT services are lower cost and lower priced than traditional media/communications | **Negative:** New revenue cannibalizes old higher unit revenue | **Positive:** Communicating and media are cheaper than ever |
| Technology innovation and product life cycles are shorter than ever | **Negative:** Return on investment (ROI) for research and development and capital outlays is declining | **Positive:** Product enhancements and new solutions come at a very rapid pace |
| Traditional infrastructure is not required | **Negative:** Incumbent media and communications companies are slow to move forward because of their infrastructure, making them less competitive against newcomers | **Positive:** Increased accessibility to IT; in China users do not even need an address for billing—people use GSM cell phones with prepaid cartridges |

Asian companies may revert to their old monopoly or oligopoly ways, which would stifle the pace and quality of IT innovations.

## Major Producers:  The "Japan" Model

In contrast to IT use in Asia, which is driven by a few differing models and factors, IT producers in Asia are surprisingly uniform. Asia's IT industry can be distilled to one primary development model:  the "Japan Model." We find that, with very few variations, all of Asia's leading IT producers can be defined in terms of which stage they are at in the Japan Model. Figure 1.3 presents the major stages of the Japan Model of IT industrial development, which can be described as a combination of Europe's top-down regulation and U.S. bottom-up entrepreneurialism. (Although this study focuses specifically on IT development, the Japan Model can be seen as a subset of the broader tendency of Asia's governments to foster industrial policy in general.)

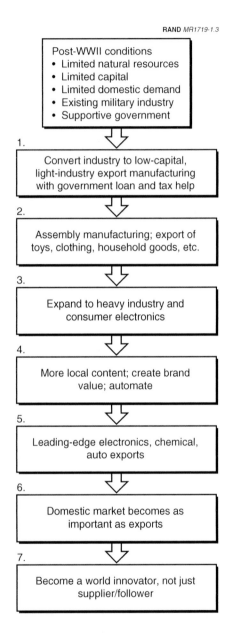

RAND *MR1719-1.3*

Post-WWII conditions
* Limited natural resources
* Limited capital
* Limited domestic demand
* Existing military industry
* Supportive government

1. Convert industry to low-capital, light-industry export manufacturing with government loan and tax help

2. Assembly manufacturing; export of toys, clothing, household goods, etc.

3. Expand to heavy industry and consumer electronics

4. More local content; create brand value; automate

5. Leading-edge electronics, chemical, auto exports

6. Domestic market becomes as important as exports

7. Become a world innovator, not just supplier/follower

**Figure 1.3—The Japan Model of the Evolution of IT Production**

Although not all countries started with Japan's set of postwar conditions, they have opted to follow Japan's development model as a "proven template" for success. In Table 1.9, seven economies have been identified as major IT producers because their IT output and export account for a substantial part of their economy, and IT is therefore a major agenda for the government and its policies. These seven all follow the Japan Model but are at very different stages.

**Stages 1 and 2.** The starting point of the Japan Model is a poor economy—either impoverished by war like Japan, Korea, and Taiwan, or simply impoverished like the Philippines, Malaysia, and Thailand 20 years ago. The lack of local demand and lack of capital means that local industry has to begin by serving overseas markets, preferably in ways where the upfront investment is very low, and raw materials and components are either cheap or supplied by the customer. To fulfill these conditions, Asian industry started out manufacturing and exporting low value-added products, such as the proverbial cocktail umbrellas, plastic toys, cheap shoes, knock-off handbags, etc. That

### Table 1.9

### Asia's IT Producers at a Glance

| IT Producer | Stage | IT Ownership | Expertise |
|---|---|---|---|
| Japan | 7 | Domestic | Consumer electronics, advanced materials and components, IC design and manufacturing; computers |
| South Korea | 6 | Domestic | Consumer electronics, phones, peripherals, IC design and manufacturing |
| Taiwan | 5 | Domestic | PCs, peripherals, components, IC design and manufacturing, some communications equipment |
| Singapore | 4 | Domestic and foreign | Disk drives, PC peripherals assembly, some IC manufacturing |
| Malaysia | 3 | Foreign | Disk drives, PC peripherals assembly, cell phone assembly |
| Thailand | 2 | Foreign | Disk drives, disk drive component assembly |
| Philippines | 2 | Foreign | Peripherals assembly, some software, services |

was the case in Japan, Taiwan, South Korea, and, more recently, China. Singapore, Thailand, Malaysia, and the Philippines started out even lower; they entered the industrial age with the labor-intensive assembly of final or intermediate products with parts that were supplied by their customers (consignment shipments).

In these early stages, government assistance is a key driver. In Japan, Korea, and Taiwan where the emerging IT industries were composed of local companies, preferential lending, grants, seed investment, subsidized land, research and development (R&D), training costs, and tax holidays were made available. In Southeast Asia where the IT industry comprises foreign entities, investment incentives, import/export conveniences, and cost subsidies were used to attract companies such as Seagate Technologies (disk drives), Hewlett-Packard, Nokia, Motorola, IBM, Philips, Acer, Samsung, Panasonic, and many others.

**Stages 3 and 4.** The next major phase comes after the local industry has accumulated some wealth and industrial expertise. Not content to simply make cheap souvenirs and household products, or to assemble portions of complex products, the regional industries reinvest to gain the know-how to produce more complex products.

In the case of Japan and Korea, they moved on to making cameras, watches, televisions, radios, and electronic toys. Basic industries also matured, such as chemicals, plastics, steel, and advanced materials, leading to increased local content. Although still considered low-value in the global IT world, these local companies began to make a name for themselves as consumer electronics manufacturers: Sony, Panasonic, Mitsubishi, Samsung, Lucky Goldstar (LG), and Acer. In Southeast Asia, control of IT remained in foreign hands, but the value-added expanded from simply assembling disk-drive boards to assembling head stacks, ICs, and final products such as monitors, printers, and mobile phones. In all areas, automation was increasingly used to ensure better uniform quality and to handle more complex precision components such as semiconductors. In northern Asia, limited labor availability and rising labor costs also necessitated greater automation.

Stages 3 and 4 are an interesting breaking point in Asia's IT development. Whereas Korea, Taiwan, and Japan passed through these phases (in the late 1970s to early 1990s) and moved on, Southeast Asia, with the possible exception of Singapore, seems to be stagnating here (see Table 1.10). Local manufacturing content has definitely increased, but there are few recognizable local IT companies and few indigenous product development or material and component industries. A key reason is that the IT industry in these countries is controlled by foreign companies who have no particular interest in transferring knowledge or developing talent. In fact, disk-drive companies such as Seagate and Maxtor move from country to country in search of the lowest-cost labor. And although workers and line managers are locally hired, senior management is invariably foreign.

Southeast Asia has also suffered from the rapid rise of China. China offers similar access to a low-cost labor pool *and* with the added attraction of a potentially vast local market in the long term. Additionally, Taiwan manufacturers, which used to rely heavily on Malaysia and the Philippines, have largely shifted to China for the common language convenience. Finally, political and economic instability have proved deadly to the fledgling IT industries in the Philippines and Indonesia.

### Table 1.10

### Development Outlook for IT Producers

| IT Producer | Chance of Advancement | Drivers | Inhibitors |
|---|---|---|---|
| Japan | High | Advanced IP market | — |
| Korea | Medium | Increasing global success | Heavy government reliance |
| Taiwan | Medium | Successfully moving up value chain | No local market; political instability |
| Singapore | Low | — | Rising cost; few risk-takers |
| Malaysia | Low | — | Labor cost rising; no local players |
| Thailand | Low | — | No local players; no English |
| Philippines | Low | — | Political instability |

Southeast Asia's inability to jump-start its own indigenous IT industry can even be seen indirectly as one of Malaysia Prime Minister
Mahathir's major career disappointments. A cornerstone of his economic and industrial policy for Malaysia is the Bumiputra Policy,
which gave preferential education, investment, and legal treatment
to indigenous Malays in hopes that foreign and ethnic Chinese business successes could be transferred, or in other words, to move
Malaysia beyond Stage 3 of the Japan Model. In recent years, Mahathir has himself expressed frustration over the policy's failure to
motivate the development of indigenous industry.[29]

The near-term prognosis for Southeast Asia is not favorable, and the
basic economics of its positioning as an IT producer relative to China
suggests that a significant change or a fresh approach is indeed
needed to avoid a long-term stagnation or decline. In Table 1.11, using GDP per capita as a general proxy for average income levels, China's relative attractiveness as a low-cost manufacturing base is obvi-
ous in 1997. China's GDP per capita then was a 32 percent discount
to Indonesia's and a stunning 84 percent discount to Malaysia's.
Given that global IT hardware demand is not sufficient to support
large factories in all of these countries, it is not surprising that in the
last five years, IT production has migrated toward the lower-cost
center of China. Hence, total GDP has fallen significantly since 1997
in Indonesia, Malaysia, the Philippines, and Thailand, whereas it has
risen in China. (The IT industry has overcapacity even in 2003, so

Table 1.11

GDP and GDP per Capita

| | GDP ($ billions) | | GDP per Capita ($) | | Population (millions) | |
|---|---|---|---|---|---|---|
| | 2001 | 1997 | 2001 | 1997 | 2001 | 1997 |
| Indonesia | 145.3 | 215.7 | 680 | 1,076 | 213.6 | 200.4 |
| Malaysia | 87.5 | 100.2 | 3,677 | 4,618 | 23.8 | 21.7 |
| Philippines | 71.4 | 82.3 | 927 | 1,154 | 77.0 | 71.3 |
| Thailand | 114.8 | 151.1 | 1,876 | 2,544 | 61.2 | 59.4 |
| China | 1,159.0 | 898.2 | 911 | 730 | 1,271.9 | 1,230.1 |

SOURCE: World Bank, World Economic Indicators Database.

---

[29]Yamazaki (2002).

every new factory comes at the expense of some existing higher-cost or less-competitive factory elsewhere.)

Considering that as of 2001, China is no longer the lowest GDP per capita country, will IT production start migrating to Indonesia and the Philippines? We believe that a strong trend in this direction is unlikely because of security concerns. Additionally, China's fast-rising per capita GDP, coupled with its huge population, now spells market opportunity. To access this opportunity, IT producers will tolerate rising costs in China to some degree to maintain a local foothold. China's population is *3.4 times larger* than all four Southeast Asian countries combined. These basic numbers sum up the overwhelming challenge that such countries as Malaysia and Thailand face. Being a low-cost producer is no longer possible (unless standards of income and living are dialed back to 1980s level, which is undesirable and politically untenable), and they have pitiable market sizes with which to attract global IT industrial interests (Malaysia's total population is not even as large as Beijing's and Shanghai's combined). Niche, locally owned, value-added industries are needed to stem the erosion of the IT industries in Southeast Asia, although it appears that the path to this future will be left to the next generation of leaders to find.

Within Southeast Asia, a possible breakout country is Singapore, although key conditions are not ripe. Singapore's IT industry has been dominated by foreign companies. The few local companies of note are all contract electronic manufacturers: NatSteel Electronics, Chartered Semiconductor, and Flextronics. Of those, the first two are government-linked companies that receive very generous investment grants, R&D assistance, subsidized land cost, and tax holidays. As contract manufacturers, they are second tier to U.S. and Taiwanese counterparts and are not used for leading-edge products or semiconductors.[30] Past attempts to improve quality or to engage in original design have not been successful. The key issues holding Singapore back are lack of local entrepreneurialism (often considered a legacy of the controlling and even repressive nature of Lew Kuan Yew's regime), a very small local market in which to try out new ideas (population of only three million), limited labor availability, and high

---

[30]Hung (2002).

operating costs. Certainly, industry stagnation will not be for lack of effort on the government's part, which has some of Asia's most unique policies, such as importing scientists and engineers from China, forcing its population to learn a nonnative language (Mandarin Chinese), and rewarding its college graduates for reproducing (to ensure propagation of their genes).

**Stage 5: Taiwan—Manufacturers Extraordinaire.** Taiwan's IT industry is an interesting hybrid of many of those already highlighted. Table 1.12 highlights Taiwan's uniqueness, as having attributes of both Southeast Asia's flexibility (represented by Singapore) and Northeast Asia's technology focus (represented by Korea).

Taiwan's IT industry is the unique OEM/ODM business model (original equipment design and manufacturing). Singapore's is primarily contract manufacturing where a customer such as Seagate

Table 1.12

Comparison of IT Industry Characteristics in Korea, Taiwan, and Singapore

|  | Korea | Taiwan | Singapore |
|---|---|---|---|
| Product design | Yes | Yes | No |
| Own brand | Yes | No | No |
| Quality/price | Medium/low | High | Medium/low |
| Business scope | Limited | Wide | Limited |
| Business model | Low price product sales | OEM/ODM | Contract manufacturing |
| Company concentration | Few conglomerates | Numerous and focused | Few and focused |
| Share of world output | Significant | Significant | Not significant |
| Financing | Debt and equity | Equity | Equity |
| Company ownership | Banks, institutions | Individual | Foreign, government |
| Key products/businesses | DRAMS, flat panels, TVs, VCRs, monitors, PCs, mobile phones | IC design, foundry, packaging, desktop and notebook PCs, motherboards, computer mouse devices, keyboards, scanners, monitors, flat panels, DRAMs, chipsets, key components, power supplies, mobile phones, switches, hubs, digital cameras, PDAs, servers | Assembly of disk drives, printers, PCs, game boxes, and other similar systems; IC foundry |

will give detailed instructions on how they want their product assembled, and will supply most of the key parts as well, or a company such as H-P will have its own subsidiary plant on site to assemble products. In Taiwan, local companies design and manufacture new models of products, and a company such as IBM or H-P will decide to buy them, attach their own label, and sell them as IBM and H-P products globally. With the exception of Acer, Taiwan companies are content to supply to global brand names rather than establishing their own as the Koreans have 'with Samsung and LG. This OEM/ODM industry comprises hundreds of companies, all equity-funded, with each specializing in a single or narrowly defined product line or expertise. For example, five companies in Taiwan make only monitors and constitute over 60 percent of the world's supply (MAG, ADI, Chuntex, Acer Peripherals, and Tatung). And seven companies make notebook PCs and constitute over 70 percent of the world's supply (Compal, Clevo, Arima, Inventec, Twinhead, Acer, and FIC). Although the average American consumer might not have heard of these companies, they certainly have bought their products, sold as Dell, IBM, Fujitsu, Toshiba, Compaq, H-P, Packard-Bell, Siemens, or another well-known brand.[31]

Taiwan has also moved up the value chain rapidly and successfully. Only ten years ago, Taiwan had to import over 80 percent of the semiconductors (ICs) it used in product manufacturing. Now, it is a net exporter of ICs; its largest semiconductor company, TSMC, is second only to Intel in annual revenues and is known as a top-quality advanced semiconductor manufacturer. Taiwan professionals are also more entrepreneurial than their Japanese, Singaporean, or Korean counterparts—numerous IT companies in Silicon Valley are founded by Taiwan arrivals, such as smaller publicly listed companies Tvia, Altigen, Trident, and Vitria, and also larger ones such as Viewsonic, ATI, and nVidia ($4 billion market capitalization).

Although there are clear fledgling signs of innovation and the ability to develop advanced technologies, Taiwan faces a significant hurdle moving beyond its current stage. The key constraint can be summed up in one word:  China. Taiwan's local IT industry faces a steady flight of both talent and capital—so although Taiwan companies

_____

[31]Market Intelligence Center press release (2002).

succeed and grow, their earnings are increasingly from offshore sub-sidiaries in places such as China and Malaysia (for manufacturing), and the United States and Europe (for product design and sales). Once a Taiwan company develops to a certain size, it starts to lower its operating risk by setting up subsidiaries abroad. Taiwan itself is not considered a desirable place to grow because of the instability arising from its adversarial relationship with China, capital movement restrictions, limited local labor resources, and limited domestic market potential. China is a popular place to establish factories because of labor availability and market potential, but the political climate can sometimes make Taiwanese investors feel vulnerable. Moreover, the lack of direct flights between Taiwan and the Mainland can make transactions somewhat inconvenient. Yet, it is estimated that 600,000 Taiwan citizens reside and work in China and that 49 percent of Taiwan companies' hardware output is actually made in China.[32] The United States, Canada, and Australia are popular overseas study destinations, and some students settle permanently. So although individuals from Taiwan continue to succeed globally, their efforts are scattered and not aggregated or concentrated in Taiwan itself, in the same manner as in Japan and Korea. The Taiwan government nonetheless comes up with a steady stream of initiatives to reinvigorate the domestic industry and market but with limited success (Taiwan companies' hardware output actually made in Taiwan fell to a low point of 38 percent in the first quarter of 2002).[33]

**Stage 6: Korea—Focused Exporters.** Korea's IT development has reached Stage 6. Its IT companies (basically three: Samsung, LG, and Hyundai) are global market share leaders, but they are very narrowly focused and definitely not innovative. For example, these three companies all engage in semiconductor manufacturing, but they basically make only one product: DRAM memory chips. Over 90 percent of their semiconductor revenue is derived from DRAM sales, and together they account for 40 to 50 percent of the global supply of DRAMs, a critical component in PCs and servers. DRAMs are a commodity, volume IC product, which are basically only price differentiated. Unique DRAM architecture developments have very

---

[32]Pao (2002).
[33]Pao (2002).

noticeably come from such design companies as Rambus in the United States or NEC in Japan.

Other product areas in which Korea figures prominently are consumer electronics (TVs and VCRs), flat panel displays, PC monitors, and mobile phones. Each of these cases is similar to the DRAM example—Korea's IT export industry is relatively narrowly focused on only a few products, but it is a major global player in each of them. The recent economic crisis in Korea has put its IT companies in a position similar to Japan's, with the big loser being Hyundai (to keep its car company alive, Hyundai has spun off most electronic divisions including disk drives (Maxtor), IC packaging (ChipPac), and DRAMs (Hynix)). Samsung and LG have soldiered on, with a new focus on mobile phones. Again, although their production rampup has been truly impressive, with such interesting product features as built-in cameras and color displays, the core technology ICs are purchased from U.S.-based design companies such as Qualcomm, Anadigics, and Motorola.

Korean firms have made clear inroads in establishing name brand and entering markets, but they are fairly uniformly viewed as low-cost competitors in each of their segments. Thus far, success in the home market has not translated well globally. A major reason is the nature of the success at home. A significant study has shown that mobile phones sell very well in Korea when the subsidy is high, and sales drop immediately when subsidies are eliminated. LG Telecom's handset sales grew by 21 percent between December 1998 and March 1999 when heavy subsidies were offered.[34] Sales dropped by 2 percent between April 1999 and June 1999 when the subsidy promotion was withdrawn. Sales then perked up by 12 percent between July 1999 and September 1999 when a partial subsidy was offered again. Korean companies have become so accustomed to operating in a regulated and closed home market that a sea change in corporate management philosophy may be needed before its IT companies can truly become global innovative leaders and compete on grounds other than price.

---

[34]Choi et al. (2000).

**Stage 7: Japan.** At Stage 7, Japan's IT industry is one of the most advanced in the world and on par in quality with that of the United States, although with considerably less breadth. Alone in Asia, Japan's IT companies have achieved a very high level of global brand recognition as innovators and leading-edge manufacturers. Japan's areas of IT excellence are heavily concentrated in equipment and manufacturing (see Table 1.13), although its most recent success story has been NTT Docomo for advanced mobile services. Certain IT subsectors have not developed at all in Japan, most notably software and telecommunications infrastructure equipment, but that does not detract from its existing competencies or its long-term ability to continue to develop and dominate in key IT markets.

As noted in Figure 1.3's depiction of the rise of Japan's IT industry, government assistance was a key element in its early establishment and still exists, although to a much smaller extent. The range of assistance has been extensive, including preferential lending, local market protection, tax benefits, and government-sponsored R&D and other costs (discussed further below). In the United States, such assistance is viewed as constituting unfair trade practices, and U.S.

**Table 1.13**

**Areas in Which Japan Leads in World Market Share or Product Excellence**

| Company | Areas of Excellence |
| --- | --- |
| Alps | Magnetic disk-drive heads |
| Canon | Cameras, IC manufacturing equipment, office equipment, optic components |
| Fujitsu | Servers, mainframes, enterprise systems, office equipment, hardware, and ICs |
| Hitachi | Enterprise systems, enterprise software, advanced ICs |
| Kyocera | Advanced chemicals and materials, electronic components |
| Matsushita | Stereos, TVs, VCRs, DVD players, office equipment |
| NEC | Advanced ICs, PCs, servers, LCD panels, office equipment |
| Nintendo | Game boxes |
| NTT Docomo | Mobile services |
| Shinkawa | IC manufacturing equipment |
| Sony | Walkman, cameras, game boxes, notebook PCs, stereos, TVs |
| Sumitomo | Advanced chemicals and materials for aerospace and electronics, power plants |
| Tokyo Electron | IC manufacturing equipment |
| Toppan Printing | Printed circuit boards, IC substrate materials |
| Toshiba | Notebook PCs, advanced ICs, LCD panels, consumer electronics |

companies and the U.S. Trade Representative have brought numerous suits against specific industries or companies in Japan, particularly in the 1980s and early 1990s.

Ironically, government assistance, which was critical to IT development initially, is now forcing Japan's industry to rethink and restructure. The practices of policy lending and of cross-subsidies[35] within conglomerates have led to such IT successes as those listed in Table 1.12 but, as it turns out, at a great cost to the overall Japanese economy. For decades, the government directed banks to lend generously and indiscriminately to critical industries such as electronics. Not all companies succeeded, and the noncompetitive ones did not go bankrupt, they simply borrowed more money. Today, it is estimated that Japan's banks have an aggregate $2 trillion in nonperforming loans, and the top 15 banks are believed to be losing more than $30 billion annually.[36]

Even on a corporate level, the system has been breaking down. As Japan's electronics and semiconductor manufacturers lost market share to aggressive Korean and Taiwanese companies, initial losses would simply be subsidized by other divisions in the conglomerate. Using money either from the government or from sister companies to prop up fundamental business failings has virtually brought Japan's economy to a grinding halt. Despite the unemployment and loss of face it entails, Japan's conglomerates are slowly, but surely, closing loss-making divisions and consolidating operations, sometimes with competitors. Large conglomerates are deciding what their true core competencies are and restructuring and streamlining accordingly. Sony has scrapped its PC division, Fujitsu is getting out of disk drives, Toshiba no longer makes DRAMs, and so on.

Getting through this phase successfully is likely to put Japan into a whole new "Stage 8," which looks much like the U.S. IT industry, where the companies are lean, focused, profit-oriented, and compet-

---

[35]*Policy lending* refers to a practice where a country's banks are directed by the government to lend to companies in specific industries as part of an overall economic policy to develop that industry rapidly; the borrower's credit-worthiness is not taken into consideration for loan approval. *Cross-subsidy* within a conglomerate is the use of one subsidiary's profits to prop up another loss-making subsidiary's operations.

[36]Overholt (2002).

ing globally with no government subsidies or support. Such companies would be a far cry from the vertically integrated IT behemoths, which relied on government help to get by. At such a stage, the IT industry will be self-sustaining, where company or entrepreneur funding is obtained from banks or the capital markets solely on the basis of the merits of the business itself, its profitability, and its competitiveness. The beginnings of this trend are already evident with the recent growing number of new listings of companies in both Japan and Korea, as the banks and governments are no longer in a position to extend easy credit. In the first half of 2002, Korea led the world markets in initial public offerings (IPOs) with 103 on Kosdaq, and Japan was second with 49 IPOs on its Jasdaq and Mother markets. If these newly independent IPO companies survive and flourish and inspire others to follow, then Japan's IT industry will have finally shed the last vestiges of government support and moved onto a new stage, similar to that in which U.S. IT companies operate.

An example of such a new stage company is NTT Docomo. It is not a complex conglomerate but one focused solely on mobile data services. After learning from and dominating the local market, NTT Docomo has been rolling out its services in new global markets, such as Germany, Taiwan, and Malaysia. It has also taken strategic investment stakes in international companies such as British Telecoms and AT&T Wireless in preparation for even larger service rollouts in the future. It is too early to tell if Japanese-style mobile surfing will be popular in international markets, but the company is certainly making all the right moves by expanding globally in its specialty area, as opposed to taking loans from the government to expand vertically or laterally at home in noncore markets.

**Watching Japan.** Korea, Taiwan, and even China watch developments in Japan closely. All three follow the Japan Model, with the same benefits and pitfalls. China and Korea in particular have a legacy of many noncompetitive companies, artificially supported by both government policy loans and sister companies. Partly because of the advance warning provided by Japan's economic woes, both countries have moved aggressively to bankrupt where necessary and put companies on "sink or swim" notice. Taiwan's banking system and economy also suffer from the burden of large nonperforming loans, which were made as part of a government development policy. However, in Taiwan's case, the IT sector is largely outside this problem because, unlike in Korea and Japan, technology companies are primarily equity funded, smaller in scale, and profitable in their core businesses.[37]

**Emerging Players—China and India.** Clearly defined clusters of IT industry are already developing in China and India, although IT output is far from being a major component of either country's economic or political concerns. They both are on course with the key components of the Japan Model. Both governments, particularly China, have policies in place to encourage foreign companies to invest and produce locally, as well as incentives and allowances to foster home-grown IT companies. They are also starting low on the value-added chain. An assortment of lower-end hardware manufacturing dominates in China, and services and software outsourcing is leading the charge in India. India's software exports have risen from $150 million ten years ago to $7.6 billion in the 12 months ending March 2002 (two-thirds are bound for the United States).[38]

China will almost surely advance to later stages in IT industry development, but India may not. The major driving force in China is the size and potential of its local market and the almost endless availability of cheap labor. China has become the manufacturing base of choice in recent years and has rapidly attracted a large knowledge base of increasingly advanced know-how. Semiconductor manufacturers believe that China will be the next great center of production and consumption.

In India, the environment simply does not seem ripe yet; software created there has negligible copyright protection, services are hard to scale, the domestic market is tiny, and manufacturing has not taken root. Political instability and a discouraging venture formation environment are added hurdles. As a result, India faces a similar problem of "brain drain" as Taiwan. Noteworthy Indian entrepreneurs

---

[37]Overholt (2002).

[38]Hua (2002).

are numerous in the United States and many have known corporate success.  In 2001, 60 percent of all H-1 visa holders (residence in the United States based on employment of a skill in shortage in the United States) in Silicon Valley were software engineers, with Indian citizens constituting 43 percent of the total (approximately 110,500 engineers).[39]

**Asia's Hardware Focus.**  A final point to note about Asia's IT industry is its heavy focus on stand-alone hardware products.  Asia has thus far entirely by-passed the enterprise solutions business, currently dominated by U.S. and European companies such as IBM, BEA Systems, Computer Sciences Corp., Oracle, Siebel Systems, PeopleSoft, SAP, Sun Microsystems, Hewlett-Packard, Cisco Systems, Lucent, EDS, Siemens, or even smaller companies such as Micromuse, Veritas, i2 Technologies, Tibco, EMC, and many others.  Asia's IT involvement up to now is primarily focused on making stand-alone, standardized, or easy-to-use products.  Essentially, Asia lacks entirely the IT services, software, and value-added consulting businesses.

Although Asia's tourism industry is world-renowned for the excellence of its service, its IT industry is not.  A prime example is Acer; Acer manufactures not only its own PCs but also IBM brand PCs, yet Acer has never been able to crack the U.S. or European markets (it has all but withdrawn from the United States).  The hardware product is no worse than comparable U.S. brands, but its service network, support, and value-added offerings are very weak.  This hurdle is likely a complex one involving many factors such as corporate culture, language, usage patterns, and value perception (Asian users believe that service and customization should come free with a product, whereas Americans readily pay an extra premium for service and customization).  The early exceptions to this rule are, yet again, found in Japan (Fujitsu and Hitachi), although they are not likely to start an Asia-wide trend anytime soon.  Asia's IT industry is likely to stick to low-cost advantages and manufacturing for the foreseeable future.  Mobile Internet and broadband are two advances pioneered in Asia, which, however, have not been successfully exported yet despite some considerable effort.

---

[39]"Regional Economic Survey: Silicon Valley" (2002).

# IT GOVERNMENT POLICIES[40]

As outlined above, government policies play a major role in the establishment and ongoing development of Asia's IT industry (and, indeed, all aspects of industry). Government policies are unanimously favorable in their intentions toward the IT industry and almost as unanimously favorable toward promoting IT use. Since the IT industry is such a critical part of most Asian economies, the governments are even somewhat competitive about offering the best investment conditions and providing the most assistance to domestic IT companies. We begin this section by discussing nine main types of government IT promotion. We then consider some of the ill effects of government promotion of IT. We conclude by briefly discussing two policy realms that fall outside the realm of promotion: deregulation and content control.

## Forms of Promotion

**Sponsored R&D.** Japan's Ministry of Economics, Trade and Industry (METI, known as MITI before 2001), pioneered a successful strategy of directly setting up government-funded nonprofit research centers to develop leading-edge and critical product, component, and process technologies, which are then transferred to companies at a very low price. This allowed companies to focus their own resources on marketing and sales for products on hand. Established in 1951, METI still funds research centers today throughout Japan and for a wide range of disciplines. This approach was copied successfully by Taiwan in 1973, with the government-funded nonprofit ITRI (Industrial Technology Research Institute), which today boasts a staff of 6,000 and 12 research divisions. One of ITRI's most noted successes was development of the semiconductor manufacturing processes that, transferred to companies, has led to Taiwan's leadership in IC production today. Korea's ETRI (Electronics and Telecommunications Research Institute), established in 1976, is similarly government-funded for its basic research in six fields of advanced technologies. China launched its National High-Tech R&D program ("863" pro-

---

[40]In Chapter Two, we take up the implications of the information revolution for government. Here, we are interested in the implications of government for the information revolution.

gram) in 1986, in which the Ministry of Science and Technology provides encouragement and funding to companies and projects in 19 priority sectors, ranging from agriculture to pharmaceuticals and advanced manufacturing. Finally, Hong Kong, hoping to foster an IT industry, announced the establishment of ASTRI (Applied Science and Technology Research Institute) in 2001 to begin research efforts with local universities in IT, biotech, electronics, and precision engineering.[41]

**Policy Lending.** As governments decide they want to foster the development of a local IT industry, banks and finance companies are directed to lend to companies in the industry, without consideration of the borrower's stand-alone credit-worthiness, and often at below-market interest rates. This has been used aggressively in Japan and Korea. Taiwan, Thailand, and Malaysia have practiced policy lending as well, but to much smaller extents, and in more limited circumstances. China has as well, but as part of the broader context of the communist state-owned enterprise system. Although policy lending had a clear beneficial effect in the early growth and establishment of the *keiretsu* and *chaebols*,[42] it is now viewed as one of the major underlying causes of the Asian financial crisis in 1997 and of Japan's ongoing recession. Policy lending still exists today, although it is primarily limited to defending from bankruptcy such old companies as Hynix in Korea, rather than seeking to grow any new companies.

**Tax Incentives.** High-tech companies in many countries in Asia can expect to get some degree of corporate income tax holiday. In China, Malaysia, and Thailand, qualifying high-tech companies are allowed a certain number of tax-free years, followed by some reduced tax years, before having to pay the regular statutory corporate tax rates. Typically, tax-free years do not start counting until after the company reaches profitability. Other governments such as Taiwan and Korea give very generous tax credits for every dollar of capital investment, R&D, or employee education spent. As a result, Taiwan's TSMC, the world's largest IC foundry and second-largest semiconductor com-

---

[41]www.meti.go.jp/english/, www.hongkong.org/ehongkong3/astri.htm, www.etri.re. kr/e_etri/, www.itri.org.tw/eng/.

[42]*Keiretsu* are Japanese conglomerates, such as Mitsubishi and Hitachi. *Chaebols* are the Korean conglomerates, such as Samsung and LG.

pany, has never paid a penny in corporate income tax in Taiwan.[43] This policy has been a popular drawing card for foreign companies looking for Asia plant sites. (Interestingly, some governments such as Hong Kong hold their tax laws to be inviolable and while many incentives are offered, taxes are never touched.)

**Free Trade Zones.** To attract export manufacturers, most Asian countries have established free trade zones, typically near ports or airports. Locating an assembly factory in such a zone means that a company does not need to officially import materials and components, which will only end up being immediately exported after assembly. Significant bureaucratic hassle is avoided and time as well as cash flow saved, since import duties do not need to be paid for the duration of the manufacturing process.

**Industrial Parks.** Most countries have created industrial parks to attract IT companies. The government takes over a large acreage, clears it, builds roads, brings in all utilities, including reliable power supplies and quality data communications, and sometimes even builds standard factories. All an IT company has to do is literally move in. Rent is usually subsidized as well. Sometimes, the industrial parks are also free trade zones or can automatically confer tax-free status on their tenants. Industrial parks are numerous throughout Asia and are considered an ideal way to generate high-quality jobs and long-term economic benefits.

**Business and Trade Development.** Aside from undertaking research, some governments also take an active role in pushing the wares of its companies. Japan's JETRO (Japan External Trade Organization) is a model example. Established in 1951, it provides Japanese companies with international market intelligence, assistance with international communications, trade shows, promotion, etc. Similar organizations include Singapore's Economic Development Board, Taiwan's Institute for Information Industry, and Korea's various ministries, which even subsidize professional fees paid for marketing and business development by Korean companies overseas.

---

[43]Taiwan Semiconductor Manufacturing Corp. annual financial statement 2001, filed with the U.S. Securities Exchange Commission.

**Grants and Investment.** The Taiwan and Singapore governments have investment funds (derived from tax revenue), which invest in companies and industries that have been designated as desirable for economic development. Notably, the government was a major shareholder in the largest semiconductor companies in both Taiwan and Singapore. The Shanghai municipal government is also an investor in China's first domestic semiconductor company. Grants are also given in many countries for distinguished advanced technology projects, such as with China's Torchlight Program. Hong Kong's largest semiconductor company, QPL, has been a major beneficiary of government research grants.

**Domestic Market Protection.** One of the most controversial policies used in Asia is domestic market protection in favor of local IT companies. This policy has taken many forms, such as import duties on competitive foreign offerings, local content requirements on sales of foreign equipment, onerous registration processes for imported equipment or software, and outright import bans. In Japan and Korea, there are few formal legal obstacles to foreign equipment sales, but domestic brands still constitute the overwhelming local market share. Trade suits and treaties such as the World Trade Organization (WTO) have helped to address some of the most egregious market inequities, but most Asian IT companies can still count on being heavily favored in their home markets.

**Government IT Spending.** Finally, governments in Asia are themselves leading purchasers of IT. As we will discuss in the next section, Australia, China, Hong Kong, Korea, and Singapore are known for their sizable e-government initiatives to modernize both internal government operations and to provide improved delivery of public services.[44] Government IT purchases are, not surprisingly, often used as a showcase for local suppliers or to promote government policies. The most noted example is China, which has a political agenda for most major purchase agreements it signs. China has been vocal in denouncing the use of Microsoft and is using its e-government initiative to demonstrate the effective use of the openly available Linux operating system.

---

[44]International Data Corp. (2002c).

## Policy Backfires

Despite the best of intentions, some of the policies listed above have had unintended negative consequences. Broadly speaking, government assistance is extended as a springboard to future success, but the initiatives that are meant to be transitional have occasionally become a crutch that stunted future development or competitiveness, as evidenced to varying extents in Malaysia (Bumiputra Policy), China (state-owned enterprises), and Japan and Korea (debt-laden *keiretsu* and *chaebols*).

As already highlighted, policy lending and subsidies have almost always backfired. Policy lending did enable the IT industries' rapid growth to a large size, but it made them ultimately less competitive overall. Firms that should have gone bankrupt were propped up, thereby reducing the country's overall efficiency and return on capital. The financial burden has also pushed the Japanese and Korean economies to their limits. China, of course, has also been addressing the same issue: state-owned and state-funded companies have been increasingly pushed to either sink or swim on their own merits. Domestic market protection has also proved to be a double-edged sword: It created a much needed market foundation for fledgling IT companies but, with some exceptions, ill-equipped the same companies to compete globally. It also led to a higher economic cost, with consumers having to pay more, or to limited product and service options.

Another major unintended negative consequence has been corruption. When there is little or no engagement between the government and industry, as in the United States, there is little room for official corruption, since every company must apply for funds on its own merits and compete for business or die. In Asia, governments are intimately connected with IT companies, serving many roles, some of which create conflicts of interest. Considering all the various policies used by governments to promote IT, officials have been acting as lenders, investors, shareholders, regulators, suppliers, customers, and partners for trade and R&D. Korea and Japan were not brought to the fiscal brink of disaster solely by the size of nonperforming loans made to uncompetitive companies. They also faced the staggering cost of payoffs made to ensure access to various loans, funds, contracts, and benefits.[45]

Finally, one well-known aspect of Japan's government "partnership" with industry is to anticipate future opportunities and to direct companies' R&D efforts accordingly. This was a great success when Japan's MITI marshalled corporate and government research efforts to make Japan a player in the global semiconductor industry in the 1970s. However, incorrect future assessments also wasted billions in actual dollars spent and in opportunity cost and lost time. Most notably was Japan's pursuit starting in 1980 of "fifth generation" computers capable of performing logical functions approaching or matching human reasoning, or in other words, in pursuit of artificial intelligence. The effort was abandoned by MITI in 1995, with no meaningful by-products or results.[46]

## Deregulating Telecommunications

Historically, the telecommunications industry in Asia was straightforward: There was only one type of service—fixed line voice, and typically one operator—which was usually state-owned by the telecom regulator or ministry. The last decade has brought major changes. First, the service types expanded to include pager service, wireless phone service, and data service, which can be further divided into business data, broadband, and Internet service. Second, Asian governments have jumped on the deregulation bandwagon to speed up penetration and enhance service quality. The coincidence of the two trends has left many countries with a confusing array of operators (Table 1.14), alliances, and tariff schedules, while governments try to walk the fine line between making affordable services widely available and ensuring reasonable, healthy rates of return for operators.

All governments have made considerable progress toward achieving a deregulated telecommunications market, with the greatest strides made in the wireless business, where there were no complicating legacy franchises or infrastructures. The relative success of the

---

[45]Overholt (2002).
[46]James (2002).

## Table 1.14
## Wireless Operators in Asia

| Japan | NTT Docomo | Singapore | SingTel | China | CMHK |
|---|---|---|---|---|---|
| | KDDI Cellular | | M1 | | Unicom |
| | J-Phone | | Starhub | Philippines | Globe & Islacom |
| Hong Kong | Hutchison | Malaysia | Telekom Malaysia | | Smart & Piltel |
| | SmarTone | | Mobikom | | Bayantel |
| | Sunday | | TRI Celcom | | Digitel |
| | C&W HKT | | Maxis | | Extelcom |
| | New World Telephone | | Time Wireless | Taiwan | Chunghwa Telecom |
| | Peoples | | Digi | | Far Eastone |
| Indonesia | Telkomsel | Thailand | TAC | | Taiwan Cellular |
| | Satelindo | | AIS | | KG Telecom |
| Australia | Optus | | Digital Phone | Korea | SK Telecom |
| | Telstra | | Satelindo | | KT Freetel |
| | Vodaphone | | Telkomsel | | LG Telecom |
| | Hutchison | | Excelcomindo | India | MTNL |
| | OneTel | New Zealand | Telecom NZ | | |
| | APT | | Vodaphone NZ | | |

SOURCE: J. P. Morgan (2001).

deregulation efforts can be seen in the surge of user bases and the growth of the new operators. Regulating ministries, which used to own the operator, have moved to sell their stakes to avoid conflicts of interest (such as in China). Rates have gone through periods of intense competition in some countries but are beginning to stabilize. Markets that are considered to have reached a competitive equilibrium (stable pricing environment) are Korea, Taiwan, Japan, and Hong Kong, whereas China and Thailand are still considered to be in the deregulating and market adjustment process.[47]

## Political Paranoia

The final element of government policies to consider is some governments' alternating attraction to, and yet apprehension about, the power of IT. The most conflicted government on this front is China. China's government has been aggressive in its deregulation of key IT industries, has steadily liberalized foreign investment policies, is itself a leading IT and Internet user, and is a keen promoter of a domestic IT industry.

However, factions within the political hierarchy are clearly uncomfortable with the unparalleled global information access and dissemination possible through the Internet. For example, two policies, on the books but inconsistently enforced, address this concern: All content posted in China must, in theory, be approved by the Ministry of Culture and by the relevant ministry for the content topic; and software used for "sensitive data transfers" must be registered with the Ministry of Information Industry. These restrictions would appear to most directly affect the development of e-commerce, which nonetheless has grown steadily in China.

These policies are two among many that have not been evenly or consistently enforced thus far. Instead, crackdowns are made in waves or sporadic campaigns. In 2002, over 2,400 of the highly popular Internet cafes were shut down temporarily in Beijing and Tianjin because of a fatal fire in one cafe. Government officials are supposedly checking that all cafes comply with safety standards and are registered before reopening them. The government is concerned

---

[47]CS First Boston (2001).

with the growing use of "subversive" content such as pornography and content from the foreign media, dissidents, and such outlawed groups as Falun Gong.[48] Internet cafes and universities are the most common Internet access points in China and the closures allow the government to enforce the installation of tracking software to monitor usage,[49] as well as to collect licensing fees, which are not regularly paid. In recent months, China's government has sporadically employed more technically sophisticated methods of censorship as well. Similar unevenly enforced restrictions have also been applied in the past to the use of satellite TV dishes. Although China and, to a lesser extent, others such as Singapore or even Hong Kong[50] will sporadically censor Internet use, they are nonetheless fully expected to push the continued proliferation of IT as a key part of economic development, which ultimately is the most important basis of political legitimacy in Asia.

## THE FUNDING OF IT

The funding of IT companies in Asia comes primarily from corporate wealth or individual wealth (these amount to the same thing in countries where companies are primarily owned by individual tycoons). The majority of all IT companies in Asia today were spun off established companies (not necessarily IT companies), or are still part of larger conglomerates, or evolved from traditional businesses. Very few were actually founded and are still controlled by entrepreneurial engineers or IT visionaries. The notable exceptions are in Taiwan, with companies such as Acer Inc. and semiconductor company Macronix International. A third major source of funding for new IT ventures is direct government investment, although that has been limited to capital-intensive semiconductor companies in China, Taiwan, and Singapore.

---

[48]For more on the topic of dissenters' use of the Internet in China, see Chase and Mulvenon (2002).

[49]Ang (2002).

[50]Hong Kong is reportedly cracking down on Internet cafes as well, closing unlicensed operators and banning 24-hour operation and customers under 16 years of age. Also reported by Ang (2002).

Venture capital basically does not exist in Asia, in the true Silicon Valley sense of independent funding of innovative concepts at an early stage. Private equity exists and is primarily invested in mid- and late-stage private companies. This could be one major reason for the lack of innovation in Asia's IT industry. In fact, many innovative and entrepreneurial Asian professionals can be found in the United States, where the financing environment is more open to new ideas.

Every major economy in Asia has a main stock market, which is often referred as the Main Board or the country's primary stock market. In most countries, there is only the primary stock market. Even in such countries as Japan, which has three stock exchanges, the primary stock market has by far the largest capitalization and highest volume of trading (in the United States, the primary stock exchange would be the New York Stock Exchange). Primary stock markets have the toughest eligibility requirements for listing and are therefore not accessible to startup or venture companies. In Asia, the primary stock markets all require a minimum of three recent years of profitable operating history as a minimum listing eligibility.

In Table 1.15, we see that a number of economies have alternative stock exchanges to the primary market (alternative markets, or exchanges other than the primary market, are often referred to as secondary markets, the best known of which is Nasdaq in the United States). These secondary markets usually have much less stringent requirements for listing. A profitable operating history is usually not required, making it possible for a startup venture company to consider listing and fund-raising on a secondary market. However, in Asia, very few secondary stock markets are of meaningful size. In the late 1990s, secondary markets sprang up in many countries for newly established companies, but with the U.S. Nasdaq collapse in 2000, very few of these markets have taken off. For example, Australia's secondary markets BSX and NSX have a total of 11 companies listed and most are livestock, vineyards, and mines. New Zealand's New Capital Market (NCM) has only ten small listings, and Thailand's Market for Alternative Investment (MAI) has only four stocks that rarely trade. The most successful secondary markets are Japan's Jasdaq and Mother, Korea's Kosdaq, Hong Kong's GEM, and Singapore's Sesdaq. IT companies are prominent in all five markets,

**Table 1.15**

**Overview of Asia's Stock Markets (Yearend 2001)**

| | Market Capitalization (U.S.$ millions) | Market Capitalization as a % of GDP | No. of Companies | Avg. Company Size ($ millions) | IT Sector % of Total | Secondary Market? | Sizable? |
|---|---|---|---|---|---|---|---|
| Australia | 414,593 | 106 | 1,434 | 289 | < 5 | Yes | No |
| China | 573,309 | 53 | 1,268 | 452 | < 10 | No | — |
| Hong Kong | 523,178 | 322 | 914 | 572 | < 10 | Yes | Yes |
| India | 228,676 | 50 | 6,500 | 35 | NA | No | — |
| Indonesia | 175,233 | 114 | 275 | 637 | < 5 | No | — |
| Japan | 2,587,782 | 53 | 2,121 | 1,220 | ~ 20 | Yes | Yes |
| Korea | 302,818 | 66 | 1,470 | 206 | ~ 20 | Yes | Yes |
| Malaysia | 131,784 | 147 | 844 | 156 | < 5 | Yes | No |
| New Zealand | 22,251 | 45 | 230 | 97 | < 5 | Yes | No |
| Philippines | 27,234 | 36 | 236 | 115 | < 5 | No | — |
| Singapore | 189,068 | 205 | 492 | 384 | ~ 15 | Yes | Yes |
| Taiwan | 294,000 | 97 | 884 | 333 | 55 | Yes | No |
| Thailand | 47,634 | 39 | 389 | 122 | < 5 | Yes | No |

SOURCES: Stock market websites.

which do not require profitable operations or more than one to two years of operating history.

Despite lacking a good secondary market for venture listings, Taiwan is one of Asia's most innovative governments when it comes to financing. Taiwan practices policy lending as in Japan and Korea, but it is administered differently so the negative consequences of large nonperforming loans have been avoided. Instead of directing banks to lend openly to any and all IT companies, Taiwan preserves the integrity of the lending process, and the government provides guarantees instead. Therefore, if an uncompetitive company fails to earn the cash flow needed to pay off its loan, it still goes bankrupt, and the government merely loses its guarantee. Nonperforming loans are therefore not accumulated, and uncompetitive companies are not allowed to hog capital and survive indefinitely. The government's SMB Guarantee Fund was established in 1974 to provide guarantees for small and medium-size businesses lacking the assets or other collateral needed to get a loan on their own. From 1974 to 1999, the fund provided guarantees for 1.7 million cases, benefiting 114,046 businesses.[51] Additionally, the government itself has acted as a venture investor through such vehicles as the China Development Fund. Since the primary concern of the fund is policy (development of advanced industries for the economy), very long-term holding periods are possible to nurture the companies to the profitability levels required for public listing and private sector financing. The Development Fund, the Guarantee Fund, and an entrepreneurial culture have made Taiwan's IT industry most like the one in the United States in structure: Numerous equity-funded stand-alone companies of all sizes and with focused businesses.

In the future, as the economies improve, many secondary Asian capital markets are in place to handle the fund-raising needs of venture. One important legacy of the last Internet boom is that secondary markets were established in Thailand (MAI), Taiwan (TIGERS), Australia (BSX, NSX), New Zealand (NSM), and Malaysia (Mesdaq). Although they are currently illiquid or unused markets, they are still likely to play a role in the future. We note in Table 1.16 that, in the past, venture capital in Asia, aside from being paltry compared to

---

[51]Yu and Chang (2001).

Table 1.16

Global Distribution of Venture Capital, 2000

| Region | Total Invested (U.S. $ millions) |
|---|---|
| United States (outside Silicon Valley) | 70,748 |
| United States Silicon Valley | 32,692 |
| Japan | 2,937 |
| Germany | 1,211 |
| France | 1,124 |
| Hong Kong | 769 |
| Singapore | 651 |
| Sweden | 560 |
| Israel | 474 |
| India | 342 |
| Finland | 217 |
| China | 84 |
| Korea | 65 |
| Philippines | 9 |
| South Africa | 3 |

SOURCE: Nash (2002).

that in the United States, gravitated toward unusual destinations. Japan and Korea are not surprising destinations given their IT industry prowess, but Hong Kong and Singapore are certainly unlikely. The key is that both places have well-established secondary stock markets, which provide a ready exit for venture investments. Venture capital, after all, is not about entrepreneurship or even IT, it is about finding ways to net a high return on capital. So no matter how interesting Taiwan's IT industry may be, it will not attract a lot of venture capital financing until early-stage companies have a market to which it can exit. For now, though, market and investor sentiment in Asia, as in the United States, is in backlash mode and is extremely resistant to startup companies. Until this changes, the IT industry will continue to be dominated in Asia by established companies and government policies, both of which are relatively conservative.

## SUMMARY POINTS

We here abstract from the preceding some conclusions regarding trends in the information revolution in the Asia-Pacific region.

## Use Trends

- Proliferation of use is primarily driven by affordability and the quality of applications relative to traditional offerings.

- Asia is developing unique solutions to many usage hurdles. Mobile Internet use has taken off in Japan, where PCs are not convenient to small home spaces. In China and elsewhere, mobile, wireless technologies are compensating for the lack of phone line infrastructure. Widespread use of Internet cafes and *PC Pangs* make access affordable. Widespread use of debit and prepaid cards have countered the lack of credit cards. Substantial local-language content is being generated in Japan, Korea, and China.

- Popular applications are distinct from those in the U.S. and European markets. Asians have gravitated toward online gaming, stock trading, instant messaging, mobile commerce, and supply chain management.

- Corporate IT use is common but not sophisticated. Key concerns are security and a lack of good economic return on high-end IT investments.

- Highly competitive IT markets (such as mobile service and Internet service provision) have spurred use but are only marginally profitable or have cannibalized high-quality traditional revenue streams.

- A digital divide is evident, separating Asia's top ten from other countries and the urban from the rural. However, IT is also seen by many in Asia as an opportunity to catch up with the West and overcome traditional lagging infrastructures and more restricted global access.

- Censorship and attempted content control are evident in a few countries but are enforced unevenly. Overall, Asian governments consider IT good for their economies.

## Production Trends

- The Asia-Pacific region is a much more significant IT producer than a consumer. IT output is a pillar industry in Japan, Korea, Taiwan, Singapore, Thailand, and the Philippines, which have all followed a Japan Model of development, starting with labor-intensive, low-value manufacturing.

- Extensive government assistance has played a significant role in fostering Asia's IT industries. Although clearly successful given Asia's large output shares, some government policies have led to competitiveness problems, corruption, and inefficiency. Companies in Korea, China, and Japan are actively adjusting to address these challenges.

- Southeast Asian IT producers appear to be stagnating in development because of their lack of indigenous IT companies and the rise of China.

- China will almost surely advance to later stages in IT industry development because of the size and potential of its local market and its cheap labor.

- India is the only breakout country with a substantial software industry (all others engage in hardware manufacturing or product design). However, India is challenged by an ongoing outflow of skilled labor.

- Asia's IT industries are primarily funded by banks, governments, and traditional industry, all of which are inherently conservative in approach. Venture financing is virtually nonexistent, and most secondary stock markets formed in the boom years are languishing along with the U.S. Nasdaq.

- Japanese, Korean, and Taiwanese companies are the most technologically advanced and diversified, but each faces unique challenges on the road to global IT innovation.

## Outlook

- Unique usage solutions and local applications may be implemented, although few are likely to export well to U.S. or European markets.

- Tension between affordable service for consumers and reasonable returns for operators will probably continue. It will be manifest in frequent government policy adjustments, volatile pricing, and a slowdown in the pace of IT innovation.

- Asia will continue to purchase state-of-the-art technologies, leap-frogging traditional infrastructure deficiencies, such as a lack of wired telephones.

- Censorship and content control will continue to be sporadic issues, but they will give way to business and economic priorities over the long term, as governments increasingly realize that their countries' economic need for international connectivity is incompatible with strict content regulation.

- IT industries in Asia will flourish as manufacturing and services continue to be outsourced from other countries. China and India will attract the lion's share of this business because of their low labor costs and potentially large markets for local sales.

- Southeast Asian producers Malaysia, Thailand, the Philippines, and Singapore have already seen their output levels decline. Their governments are looking for solutions, which in itself is not a promising sign.

- Innovative global market leadership will remain elusive for Asia's leaders in the short term, and success may require further weaning from their home-supported ways of doing business.

- Governments have backed off the more aggressive support practices such as policy lending and local market protection. However, they continue to exert influence as they engineer deregulation of telecommunications.

- IT industry financing will come from traditional venues for the foreseeable future, with leading-edge innovators continuing to flock to the United States for their starts.

# Chapter Two

# POLITICAL IMPLICATIONS OF THE INFORMATION REVOLUTION IN ASIA

*Nina Hachigian*

This chapter addresses two interrelated questions—how has IT changed political dynamics within the countries of the Asia-Pacific region? And how are governments using IT to govern? To answer the first, which requires investigation of political dynamics, we look largely at the "bottom-up" actions and initiatives of citizens, civil society, nongovernmental organizations (NGOs) and political parties, from organizing protests of government policies to overthrowing sitting regimes. In answering the second question, we will examine "top-down" initiatives of governments that use technology to deliver information and services, generally termed electronic government or e-government. The division between these two topics is not always rigid nor, as we will see, is there necessarily a correlation between the two phenomena in a given country. Singapore, a country whose internal political dynamics have been little altered by information and communication technologies, is a world leader in e-government, for example.[1] We will examine these two topics looking separately at one-party dominant states, where a ruling party uses restrictions on communication to retain power, and at liberal democracies in Asia.[2]

---

[1] We will focus primarily, but not exclusively, on politics and governance within nations, because despite all the predictions about the decline of the nation-state, the lives of most people are still governed by their local polities. Discussion of cyberwarfare is beyond the scope of this report. See Arquilla and Ronfeldt (1996, 1997).

[2] For the purposes of this report, we distinguish between liberal democracies (that is, democracies that guarantee individual rights for citizens, particularly freedom of expression and assembly) on the one hand and "one-party dominant" states on the

We might expect that the effect of IT would be different in these different political contexts—common wisdom holds that IT will undermine closed regimes and even encourage democratization.[3] As we will see, however, hard and fast distinctions cannot be made between the political effect of IT on closed versus open regimes.[4] IT has sometimes had a significant political effect on both.

## BOTTOM UP: THE EFFECT OF IT ON INTERNAL POLITICS

The rise and spread of information technology in a society has the potential to alter power relationships between citizens and their state. Politics and governance rely on the communication of messages and ideas, and technology can bolster political power by influencing the speed, destination, and anonymity of those communications. IT is never the sole motivator for political flux, but a medium by which it occurs. Nevertheless, "technology is one of the significant causes of social and political change."[5] Harnessing IT may alter the momentum in a political contest, and a shift in momentum can become a shift in political reality.

IT can affect the internal politics of a state in several ways. For example, IT can make it easier for fringe political parties, NGOs, or dissenters, whether formally organized or not, to challenge a ruling party or a given policy by distributing messages broadly and by allowing supporters to organize easily. When information flows more freely, citizens can more easily gather facts with which to hold leaders accountable, particularly when the traditional media will not challenge the government. When opposition groups harness its transgressive power, IT can actually assist in regime change by facilitating the distribution of criticisms and protest venues.

---

other. The latter category describes countries where a ruling party has retained power for generations and includes a range of countries from "electoral" or illiberal democracies, such as Singapore, to true dictatorships, such as North Korea. Liberal democracies in Asia also vary in their openness to vigorous competition for alternative political parties, with Japan being on the less-encouraging end of the spectrum.

[3]For more on the thesis that IT promotes democratization, see Hill and Hughes (1998, p. 2). See also Kedzie (1996).

[4]See Kalathil and Boas (2003).

[5]Nye (1999).

Politics in different Asia-Pacific countries have felt the IT revolution in a variety of ways. In some Asian countries, IT has already clearly influenced political events. In others, IT has not affected politics noticeably at all. In yet others, a future influence is highly likely. We look first at the one-party dominant states in Asia.

## One-Party Dominant States: IT Influenced

The internal politics of some current and former Asia-Pacific one-party dominant states, such as Indonesia, China, and Malaysia, have clearly been influenced by IT. Other such regimes, such as North Korea, Myanmar, and Singapore, have not been the locus of notable political activity enhanced by information and communications technology (ICT). For one-party dominant states, the Internet and IT pose a paradox they must resolve—they offer enticing commercial advantages yet can empower dissent and threaten regimes by giving citizens access to new information and a platform for discussion. Controls that limit the Internet's political potential also reduce its commercial value.[6]

**Indonesia.** The most dramatic example of information technology's political effect on an Asia-Pacific dictatorship is Indonesia, where IT contributed to the downfall of President Suharto.[7] In the last years of his 30-year reign, "the Internet was used extensively by the urban middle-class opposition to get around the regime's censorship of broadcast media."[8] For example, the news magazine "Tempo," banned in 1994, found an eager online audience for the website it created in 1996, "Tempo Interaktif."[9] Estimates are that in the first six months of the site, 10 percent of the Indonesian online population had logged in. In addition to news sites, listservs became a popular medium for political discussion. One in particular, *apakabar,* organized by a professor at the University of Maryland,

---

[6]See Hachigian (2001, pp. 118–133).

[7]Indonesia was not the first country where IT had a hand in regime change. Organizers in Thailand were the first in Asia to use cell phones to generate a political movement. In 1992, cell phones, although not widely used at that time, played a role in organizing the street protests to challenge Thailand's military coup. See Zunes (2000).

[8]Sen and Hill (2000, p. 194); see also Wong (2001, p. 385).

[9]http://www.tempo.co.id.

carried passionate political discussions as well as detailed descriptions of events in Indonesia, such as the arresting of political activists, more quickly and often more accurately than the traditional media. The power of this online assembly was revealed first in 1995 when a legal aid organization working in Indonesia posted an "urgent action" message that decried the death of a labor activist in East Java, whose death many attributed to the military. Within hours of its posting, hundreds of pages of faxes poured in from around the world to the Office of the President, the Department of Defense, and the Department of Foreign Affairs. The village girl from East Java became a workers' heroine.[10]    A few years later, when political momentum for Suharto's ouster had reached a critical point, students used the Internet to "plan their moves" in the massive nationwide demonstrations that lead to the regime's collapse in 1998. Students occupying the parliament building used laptops to send messages to the outside world.[11]   Sen and Hill postulate that it was not just the utility of the Internet as a political platform that made it a popular tool of opposition groups, but that "the very freedom of the Internet became a constant reminder of the absence of openness and freedom in other media."[12]

Although Internet penetration was then and is still now relatively low in Indonesia, several factors allowed the net to empower those in opposition to Suharto. First, many Indonesians share passwords and accounts, thus reducing costs to get online. Second, Internet cafes, or "warnet," were starting to become popular and brought affordable access. There are now some 2,000 such cafes in Indonesia.[13]   Some proprietors helped their clientele locate the opposition sites. Government-sponsored public Internet kiosks also multiplied. Third, the traditional media covered much of the online political discussions, thus both advertising the existence of the forums and carrying their message. Last, the Indonesian government was not willing or able to censor the online political activity. It wanted, as many other Asian countries, to encourage the information economy and did not

---

[10]Wong (2001, p. 384).

[11]Sen and Hill (2000, pp. 194, 200). See also Marcus (1998).

[12]Sen and Hill (2000, p. 210).

[13]Purbo (2002).

have the technical or legal structures in place to block sites or monitor e-mail traffic.[14]

**China.** IT has also influenced politics in China, albeit in a more nuanced way.[15] China is unique in the Asia-Pacific region—no other government is attempting to both encourage and control IT as completely.[16] Because the Chinese Communist Party (CCP) realizes that it must sustain economic growth to keep its hold on power, the government is promoting information technology growth of every variety, investing billions in infrastructure, and encouraging competition in the telecommunications industry. The Tenth Five Year Plan for the economy issued in 2001 even mentions the importance of "popularizing" information technology. At the same time, the government blocks Internet users from accessing certain political websites based overseas and encourages a high degree of self-censorship among domestic commercial websites through a plethora of strict regulations.[17] A number of activists, academics as well as ordinary citizens, have been arrested for voicing anti-party ideas on the Internet. Moreover, any formal, organized challenge to the political authority of the CCP, online or off, is forbidden. Thus, unlike in 1990s Indonesia, technology is not used widely for antiregime political organizing in China because there is little such activity.

Despite these measures, the Internet in China is a much more free and pluralistic medium than traditional newspapers, magazines, and TV. Ideological challenges to government policies abound on the Internet, although most users are not seeking subversive political information. And to the extent that there have been, in the recent past, attempts to organize political parties, as in the case of the now-outlawed China Democracy Party, the Internet did play a critical role. Political dissenters based outside China and spiritual groups such as

---

[14]Sen and Hill (2000, p. 205).

[15]A number of writings offer full discussions of the Internet in China, among them Foster and Goodman (2000); Kalathil and Boas (2003); Hachigian (2001); Hartford (2000); Harwit and Clark (2001); Qiu (1999/2000); and Guo (2002).

[16]For more on the thesis of China being unique, see Hachigian (2002, pp. 41–58). For more on the media in general in China, see Lynch (1999).

[17]For a discussion of the role of U.S. corporations in abetting censorship, see Gutmann (2002).

the Falun Gong also make sophisticated use of IT.[18]  Underground dissident journals such as *The Tunnel* and *VIP Reference* forward their publications to hundreds of thousands of Chinese e-mail accounts from the United States.  Because authorities disperse any such efforts before they reach the point of gathering any popular momentum for political or social change, no concrete political effect from these activities is evident.

Although dissidents are not gaining much traction, Chinese political dynamics, at the central and local levels, are nonetheless being altered by IT.  The potentially most powerful political effect of increased technology access in China comes not from ideological challenges, but from ordinary citizens with an increased ability to hold their government accountable.  Information about what their governments do (and do not do) is more freely available online, and Internet forums offer a place in which to discuss such information safely.  Websites and bulletin boards that encourage discussions of political topics such as corruption, pollution, women's rights, and HIV have created a new public sphere for political discussion.  A survey by the Chinese Academy of Social Sciences has found that users in China do view the Internet as a forum to express their political opinions and as a source for political information.[19]

An example of this phenomenon occurred when a school in rural Jiangxi province exploded in March 2001, killing 38 children.  The local officials claimed that a lunatic suicide bomber caused the blast.  But regional tabloids and foreign media reported what they heard from parents—that firecrackers that the children were being forced to make to supplement the school's income had exploded.  People read these accounts on the web and discussed them in chatrooms.  "They want to cover up the child labor and the use of schools as workshops, so they have found a dead man as a scapegoat," one posting said.  When discussions became too heated, the forums were shut down.  By then it was clear that the story was beyond the control of the state media, however, and then-Premier Zhu Rongji issued an extremely rare apology.  A similar incident occurred in July 2001

---

[18]For a detailed look at the issue of dissent and the Chinese Internet, see Chase and Mulvenon (2002).

[19]Guo and Bu (2001).

when local officials tried to cover up facts surrounding a flood at a mine in Guangxi. Local reporters, who could not cover the story themselves for fear of government reprisal, e-mailed their version of events to regional papers, which began to report on the hundreds of casualties. Eventually the central government sent an investigative team that led to the arrest of the mine owner.[20]  Because fighting corruption is a major priority of the central government in China, it does not often make an effort to hide these incriminating stories about local officials.

Regime criticism is also directed at the central government. The Hainan Island spy plane incident in 2001, in which a Chinese pilot died and an American flight crew was held by China for 12 days, prompted strong anti-American but also anti-Beijing sentiment. Until censored, chat-room visitors chided their leaders for being "soft" and too old. These sorts of incidents are rare so far, but they illustrate the power of information technology to spread quickly politically sensitive information that can be used against governments. They show how Internet is "crystallizing public dissatisfaction with government."[21]

In the long run, at times of crisis, this dynamic could facilitate political change. If China's strong economy falters badly, or some other incident triggers a major political disruption, IT would make the story almost impossible to contain. Citizens could learn what foreign media were reporting about the incident and could talk to each other online in a way that would have been impossible earlier. If momentum for protests built up, e-mail would make them easy to organize. And unlike at Tiananmen Square in 1989, the country would learn how authorities handled the protesters.

**Malaysia.** Malaysian citizens are also looking to the web for accurate information on political events. The Barisan Nasional Party has ruled since 1969, and because the regime controls the traditional media very tightly, citizens search the Internet for information. Unlike in China, though, the Malaysian government has decided not to censor the Internet for the most part. The government has pinned its

---

[20]For more analysis on the powerful combination of media loosening and technology in China, see Kalathil (2002).

[21]Kalathil and Boas (2003).

hopes for the growth of its mostly market-driven economy on information technology and the Internet. Prime Minister Mahathir bin Mohamad has promoted the "knowledge economy" as a centerpiece of his regime and has invested millions in the "Multimedia Super Corridor" (MSC), Malaysia's answer to Silicon Valley. It promotes and enables Internet access, even for the poor, and places few or no restrictions on online political content. To ensure that no policy would hinder IT growth, the Malaysian government made a clear, public decision, codified in the MSC "Bill of Guarantee," not to censor the Internet, including foreign websites. Although the Malaysian government carefully controls all print and television media, and journalists who write stories criticizing the regime risk their careers, local independent online political journals, such as Malaysiakini.com, have been repeatedly harassed by the police but not shut down. Columnists who were banned from mainstream media find a professional home with these virtual journals. Such sites, frequented by average white collar workers,[22] generate independent reporting that "would not be tolerated in any of the mainstream media," including stories that criticize the ruling coalition's policies and reveal scandals.[23] Malaysiakini has become "an institution for Malaysians seeking information on the Malaysian political system."[24] Their stories embarrass the ruling coalition and possibly erode support for the party. Thus, Malaysiakini leaders question how long the government will keep its promise not to censor the Internet.

Dissident groups and NGOs also use the web in Malaysia. When Prime Minister Mahathir fired his reform-minded deputy, Anwar Ibrahim, in 1999 and imprisoned him on dubious charges, dozens of pro-Anwar sites sprung up, many hosted in the United Kingdom and the United States, to organize international condemnation. NGOs in Malaysia have used international listservs to organize campaigns to pressure the government on human rights issues, including the struggle of the indigenous peoples in Sarawak.[25] Although IT has not been responsible for a dramatic political shift in Malaysia, the media

---

[22]Wong (2001, p. 385).

[23]Chin (2001).

[24]Wong (2001, p. 386).

[25]Wong (2001, p. 381).

and others' use of the Internet has certainly changed the tenor of political dynamics and has created a channel and audience for any future political movement.

## One-Party Dominant States:  Little IT Influence

IT does not necessarily alter politics in closed regimes. There are a number of one-party dominant states in the Asia-Pacific region where IT has had no major effect.

**Myanmar and North Korea.** Myanmar and North Korea have been successful in controlling the Internet, as they do all other media, very strictly. They do so in large part by restricting access to IT. In North Korea, Internet access is illegal. No Internet service providers and no North Korean servers allow citizens to access the Internet.[26] (North Korea, however, does vigorously promote computer literacy and has opened one Internet cafe for foreigners.)  The current regime in Myanmar, the State Peace and Development Council (SPDC), has made unauthorized use of a computer or modem punishable by 7–15 years in jail.  Recently, one government-controlled Internet cafe opened in Yangon, but exorbitant membership charges prevent all but about 600 citizens from having e-mail accounts. Few people in either country have mobile phones. There are also complete restrictions on political organizing of any kind. Thus, civil society and political parties, to the little extent they may exist inside North Korea and Myanmar, are not using technology for political change. This situation could change if either country were to open up their economies in an effort to promote growth. Now that countries must compete for highly valuable but mobile and often fickle foreign capital, countries without IT infrastructure and Internet access will have great difficulty winning over investors.

Despite the controls within Myanmar, opposition groups based outside the country, many in Thailand, have been increasingly active. These groups, supplied with laptops and Internet connections by international democracy-promotion organizations, have linked with other campaigners around the world "to form a transnational movement that has pressured the SPDC to an extent many assert

---

[26]"North Korea Online This Year" (2001); Lee (2000, pp. 25–60).

would have been impossible without Internet use."[27]  An umbrella organization, the Free Burma Coalition, has used grassroots online organizing to pressure the U.S. government to impose sanctions and convince large corporations to withdraw from Burma.  It is unclear whether these efforts have had a notable political effect within Myanmar, but they have certainly affected the international debate.

**Vietnam.**  Vietnam is pursuing a strategy similar to that of China— allowing IT but attempting to control its influence.  Internet cafes have been blossoming by the thousands in urban Vietnam, and "doing the chat" is popular among teenagers.  Yet, the government built a firewall beginning in 1998 that reportedly blocks well over 3,000 political and pornographic sites.  Authorities shut down offending websites and have arrested individuals for posting articles about democracy.  The government is now considering penalties for cafe owners who allow customers to visit antigovernment or porno- graphic websites.  Although antiregime discussions among Viet- namese and the diaspora are commonplace, it is unclear what the political import of those discussions will be.[28]

**Singapore.**  IT has not had an effect on politics in the illiberal democ- racy of Singapore either.  Singapore, ruled by the People's Action Party since 1959, is not restricting IT in the least.  In fact, the gov- ernment is encouraging, even forcing, its population to adopt infor- mation technologies.  As mentioned earlier, per-capita use of the Internet in Singapore is very high.  But government controls and political apathy have teamed to make Singapore cyberspace fairly apolitical.  Just as the government closely controls all traditional media, it also keeps careful watch on any online political activity.  In 1996, the Singapore Broadcast Authority (SBA) issued the Internet Code of Practice, which prohibits all material on the Internet that might threaten the "public interest, public morality, public order, public security, [and] national harmony" or that "offends against good taste and decency."  Regulations make website hosts legally responsible for any content that appears on their sites.  ISPs must

---

[27]See Kalathil and Boas (2003).

[28]See Dang (1999); also http://www.interasia.org/vietnam/dang-hoang-giang.html; "Vietnam to Crack Down on Net Access" (2002); also http://www.guardian. co.uk/internetnews/story/0,7369,775745,00.html.

register with SBA but "are not required to monitor the Internet or its users."[29] These regulations encourage self-censorship, but the SBA claims that it "has not taken action against anyone for objectionable content on the Internet." A few widely publicized incidents in the 1990s revealed, however, that the government had been monitoring individual web browsing.[30] Current policy states, "SBA does not regulate personal communications, such as Internet Relay Chat (IRC) and e-mail. It does not monitor individual access to Web pages." Recently, with the presence of opposition parties growing on the Internet, and the then-approaching November 2001 elections, the government drafted new rules to allow closer monitoring of political websites.

Nevertheless, opposition party websites do exist and do carry criticisms of the ruling party. A few NGOs also host independent political websites that likewise post critiques of government policies.[31] But "these sites have a long way to go before they may be in a position to make some significant impact on the political scene."[32] Thus, in the near term, it is unlikely that the Internet and IT generally will, as Oehlers has said, "engender any process of fundamental political change" in Singapore.[33] This is as much due to a lack of interest in political activism on the part of the general population as to government control of political activity. As one journal commented, "Singapore is a safe, modern, high-rent enclave in an increasingly dodgy neighborhood. Why fool around with opposition politics?"[34]

## Liberal Democracies

IT has played a role in the politics of liberal democracies as well as in the one-party dominant states of the Asia-Pacific region.

---

[29]http://www.sba.gov.sg/internet.htm.

[30]Wong (2001, p. 383).

[31]Oehlers (2001). Sintercom, a popular nonprofit, uncensored, online forum, closed down in part because the editor was dismayed at broad content regulations that left him vulnerable to government prosecution. How (2001).

[32]Oehlers (2001).

[33]Oehlers (2001); see also Kalathil and Boas (2003).

[34]"No Laughing Matter" (2001).

**Philippines.** The most profound example of IT's role in an Asian democracy comes from the Philippines where, as in Indonesia, IT has been credited with a role in actual regime change. Even before the corruption accusations against then-President Estrada began to surface in 2000, text messaging and the Internet had become channels for political debate and organization among citizens. Websites that criticized and poked fun at his regime—some 200 by one estimate—proliferated soon after Estrada took power.[35] Civil society groups, such as the Philippine Center for Investigative Journalism (PCIJ), posted on their website detailed reports in the summer of 2000 on conflicts of interest in President Estrada's finances. Another well-known site, e-Lagda.com,[36] initiated a cyber petition that aimed to collect a million signatures in 21 days for the ousting of Estrada.[37] Although it gathered only 115,000 names, the effort established a group of connected and dedicated citizens who were ready to respond when the political climate became receptive a short time later. Listservs likewise came into their own as a political medium in the Philippines around the Estrada controversy. Dozens of lists circulated commentary, jokes, poems, satire, pictures, and essays focused on Estrada's removal, before such opinions surfaced in the traditional media.[38] The participants were largely ordinary Filipinos, although the worldwide diaspora also joined in. Observers note that other than the President's official website, the pro-Estrada voices on the Internet were all but silent.

Most important to the actual organization of protests were mobile phones.[39] Mobile phone penetration is high in the Philippines and text messaging is a wildly popular application, with many millions of messages sent each day.[40] Filipinos were swapping thousands of jokes and slogans about President Estrada through their handsets well before the Senate impeachment trial got under way in early

---

[35]Pabico (2000).

[36]"Lagda" means "signature."

[37]www.elagda.com.

[38]Eder (2001, pp. 23–24).

[39]See Guest (2001).

[40]"Digital Divide" (2001).

2001.[41]  Some of the websites that hosted anti-Estrada discussions added text messaging to their distribution channels.  Then, in January 2001, when a committee of senators voted to keep sealed financial evidence widely believed to be incriminating of Estrada, the public began to gather at a historic shrine less than an hour later. Anti-Estrada forces relied on text messaging to organize these efforts—sending out details of planned gatherings—meeting times, locations, and proper attire.  Eventually, as many as a million citizens joined the protests, and Estrada stepped down less than a week later. One mobile phone company found its daily average jump by nearly 60 percent to 70 million a day during the week of protests,[42] and other estimates put the total over the four-day period at 160 million per day.  Some companies had to supplement their equipment with mobile cell sites to continue providing reliable service.  As one text message that was widely circulated after the ouster put it: "CONGRATULATIONS!  THANK U 4 SUPPORT N DS HSTORICL EVENT. [ESTRADA] WIL GO DOWN N PHIL. HSTORY S BEIN D 1ST PRESIDNT OUSTD BY TXT."[43]

In the case of the Philippines, the various technologies reinforced one another—websites and listservs built a community, text messaging and e-mail organized the community, and TV images motivated the community.   IT certainly changed how events transpired, although it likely did not change the ultimate outcome.  Now "cyberactivism," as one Filipino commentator dubbed it, continues in the Philippines. Even local candidates develop websites and many send out campaign text messages, although the number they can send is limited by election laws.[44]  A number of independent election sites host discussions of candidates and issues, and sites such as PCIJ's continue to investigate and publicize possible government corruption.[45]

---

[41]Williamson (2000, p. 4).

[42]Bagalwis (2001).

[43]Bagalwis (2001).

[44]Bariuad (2001). See also www.akbayan.com for an example of a citizen's movement website.

[45]Pabico (2001).

**Indonesia.** In Indonesia, with the transition to a democratic system now complete, political parties still use the Internet. But because of the media freedom that has come with democracy, and the still low percentage of users, it is not as critical a technology to internal politics as it was in the transition period when Suharto was ousted. Activists, students, and NGOs, however, have continued to use the Internet to rally the international community, as Burmese activists have. A leader of a separatist group in Aceh recently argued that the Internet is the only way his independence movement can communicate with international powers, a critical factor for success.[46] David Hill argues that the independence of East Timor was also aided by an international network of human rights and other civil society organizations, student groups, and hackers. Operating through newsgroups, listservs, websites and e-mail, they coordinated with East Timorese leaders to publicize human rights abuses by the Indonesian military and attacked Indonesian government websites, using the "sophisticated tool" of the Internet to turn the world's shame about East Timor into a "political victory."[47]

**South Korea.** In South Korea, a democracy with now expansive media freedom and very high Internet penetration, the 2002 Presidential election became a textbook example of the power of IT. Analysts argue that the success of Roh Moo-hyun was "largely due" to his Internet-based supporters' organization, called "Nosamo."[48] With 80,000 members, the group was able to raise more than $7 million over the Internet and bring thousands to campaign rallies with text messaging, without the typical payments for lunch or bus fare. Half a million visitors logged onto Roh's site every day. A Korea University political scientist who followed the elections said "It is almost a cultural revolution."[49] Internet voting was also tested. The ruling Millennium Democratic Party sanctioned voting via Internet in the party primary for a small portion of eligible votes.

The April 2000 national parliamentary elections were an earlier example of IT's political influence. Six hundred small civic groups

---

[46]Hill (2002, p. 25).

[47]Hill (2002, p. 25).

[48] "MDP Begins Internet Voting for Presidential Primary" (2002).

[49]Demick (2003).

banded together to press the National Elections Commission (NEC) to release criminal records of all the candidates. When the NEC did so, on its official website, the umbrella group used the information to create a "blacklist" of 86 candidates, many of whom were revealed to have serious criminal records. The NEC site registered 1.1 million visitors on election day, according to the supervising official who called the response "explosive" and "beyond our imagination."[50] Importantly, although the mainstream papers did not report the damaging information at first, once the information was widely available on the Internet, they did. In the end, 58 of the 86 blacklisted candidates, including some with well-established careers, lost their contests. The coalition organizers concluded that the collaboration of groups was possible only through "meetings" on the Internet, and one analyst who followed the race closely stated that without the Internet, the coalition's effect would have been "very much limited."[51] Finally, South Korean NGOs, thousands of them, lobby the government for various policies, often using the Internet as a base and connecting with NGOs abroad.

**Japan.** As in the case of closed regimes, there are a number of democracies in Asia where IT has not had a discernible effect on politics. In Japan, despite its leadership in technology production, the Internet and other new technologies have not yet been greatly influential in politics. This reflects a general lack of dynamism in Japanese politics as the ruling Liberal Democratic Party (LDP) has a firm grip on power. One impediment has been the 1950 law that governs elections, which has been interpreted to prohibit online campaigning. A government task force is evaluating that policy and will likely recommend changes. Despite the ban, 78 percent of Diet members from eight major political parties have established websites. To comply with regulations, they do not update the sites during election season.[52] Another factor that contributes to the lack of IT influence in Japanese politics is the disproportionate influence of rural voters who have less Internet access. An incipient exception to the otherwise sleepy state of IT influence on politics might be the activism of NGOs in Japan. In one case, for example, Japanese con-

---

[50]Struck (2000). See also Chon (2000).

[51]Struck (2000).

[52]"Govt, LDP May OK Internet Campaigns" (2002).

sumer groups opposed to genetically modified foods have established websites to promote their view and have used the Internet, in part, to organize coordinated rallies across Japan.[53]

**India.** In India, as we will see in the following section, local governments have made impressive strides in using technology, especially for a relatively poor country. However, at this stage, technology has not played an influential role in India's politics. Many of the large political parties do have websites, and some of them are updated frequently. But parties are not using the Internet or other advanced technology to mobilize citizens or to gather input from them in part because IT penetration is quite low among the general population. NGOs appear to be using the web, as in other Asian countries, to network with international counterparts and to raise awareness of certain policy issues. For example, according to one account, in 2001, an Internet-based campaign by India's grassroots organizers and a network of environmental activists in Maine managed to redirect 20 tons of mercury headed for India back to the United States.[54]

**Australia.** Australia's political parties are using the Internet, but the effects of this trend are not yet significant. Although many parties have robust informational sites, there is little evidence to indicate that the parties are using IT to interact with potential supporters or in other innovative ways. As Gibson and Ward have concluded "[d]espite our high hopes for levels of web campaigning in Australia, it would appear that the parties have failed to seize the initiative. [Their] sites [do] too little to engage with users, acting more as futuristic posters than interactive gateways. . . . While a 'wired' citizenry may be a prerequisite for active online politicking, it is clearly not sufficient."[55] There are a number of independent efforts to foster a public dialogue on policy issues using the web as a convenor.[56] It is unclear at this point whether these efforts will generate a meaningful dialogue that might otherwise not have taken place. As we will see

---

[53]Takada (1999).

[54]"Internet Activism in Asia" (2002).

[55]Gibson and Ward (2002).

[56]See, for example, www.onlineopinion.com.au, www.apprn.org, and www.crikey.com.au.

below, Australia has taken the lead on some aspects of e-government and e-democracy.

## Analysis and Future Trends

Technology does not discriminate by regime type in its influence. Technology has contributed to regime change in Indonesia and the Philippines, helps Chinese citizens hold their government more accountable, affects the international debate on Myanmar, empowered the East Timorese independence movement, and is changing elections in South Korea. IT has had a strong effect in select authoritarian and democratic regimes and no effect in others (see Table 2.1).

What are the drivers of IT's influence on politics in the Asia-Pacific region? More research is needed to draw definitive correlations, but some preliminary observations are possible. First, and obviously, some degree of flux in the underlying politics of a state must be present before IT can have an effect on changing politics. In a country with staid politics, for whatever reason, be it a democracy such as Japan, where bureaucracy is so thick that it resists any change, or a dictatorship such as North Korea, where the regime allows no political challenges, or an illiberal democracy such as Singapore, where neither the regime nor the populace seems to crave change, IT will have little political effect because there is no underlying political movement. A second condition that must be met for IT to have an effect on politics is some degree of technology penetration, at least among the middle class. In every Asian country, some more than

Table 2.1

### IT Influence on Politics, by Government Type

| Influence of IT on Politics | Type of Government | |
|---|---|---|
| | One-Party Dominant States | Liberal Democracies |
| Visible influence | China Indonesia Malaysia | Philippines South Korea |
| No significant influence | Myanmar North Korea Singapore | Australia India Japan |

others, the "digital divide" is large. But when the middle class has access, citizens can use those channels for political change, as they did in Indonesia and the Philippines. Last, government controls of the media have a bearing on the political effect of IT. In such countries as Myanmar, where not only is access limited but those few with access to the Internet can surf only a list of preapproved sites, there is little room for political activity. Although it restricts online content somewhat, China nevertheless permits citizens to engage in political activity on the web if they stop short of calling for an end to the regime.

We also observe that a frequent presumption about one-party dominant states—that all are trying to control the Internet as much as possible for fear of its political effect—is not true (see Table 2.2). As we have seen, one-party dominant states are responding to IT in a wide variety of ways. At one extreme, North Korea and Myanmar are attempting to exclude the Internet. On the other end of the spectrum is Malaysia, which is encouraging its spread and not censoring its use. China and Singapore are adopting compromise approaches. It is not clear that one-party regimes that welcome IT are more likely in the long run to be undermined than those regimes that exclude it.

Table 2.2

**Degree of Restrictions on Internet Political Use and Content, by Type of Government**

| Severe Restrictions on Online Political Content and Use, Through Limits on Access | Significant Restrictions on Internet Access or Online Political Content and Use, or Both | Moderate Restrictions on Political Content and Use; Promotion of Public Internet Access | Negligible Restrictions on Online Political Content and Use; Promotion of Internet Access |
|---|---|---|---|
| *Myanmar* *North Korea* | *China* *Vietnam* | *Singapore* | Australia India Indonesia Japan *Malaysia* Philippines South Korea Thailand |

NOTE: One-party dominant states are shown in italics; liberal democracies are in normal type.

The economic growth that IT can generate may benefit a sitting regime more than the increased political opportunities of its citizens will hurt it. That is certainly true for Singapore. Malaysia and China are also taking this bet, hoping that liberalizing cyberspace will lead them to a future like Singapore, not Suharto's Indonesia.

In Asian countries with sizable IT penetration, at least among the middle class, IT will no doubt play a role in future moments of political crisis or disjuncture. This is especially true in countries where the likelihood both of significant political disruptions and of technology penetration is high, such as in China and Malaysia. Also, if closed regimes that have excluded IT, such as Myanmar and North Korea, attempt to open their economies to stimulate growth, they will have to permit IT, and then they may experience disruptions as their disenchanted populations find national and international online communities. In addition, IT will be used increasingly by NGOs to bring domestic and international pressure to bear for certain policy changes. As in every other region of the world, the international community will have an increasing influence in internal Asian politics, as the examples of Myanmar and East Timor reflect. Finally, political parties in the liberal democracies will likely increase their use of IT, but this effect will be sporadic and will depend upon the rise of political challengers that eschew traditional channels.

## TOP DOWN: GOVERNMENTS USING IT

In addition to the sometimes profound changes IT has enabled in bottom-up politics, IT is also reshaping the way Asia-Pacific governments conduct the business of government. Trends in e-government are what this section will examine.

Since the mid-1990s, countries from every corner of the earth have embraced IT. Technology was often portrayed as a miracle cure for all the many ills of government. IT, it was argued, would singlehandedly save money, bring government closer to more people, increase transparency, and reduce corruption. This enthusiasm has gradually given way to a more sober assessment, and currently most agree that "[IT] is a tool, potentially powerful yet essentially no different from a photocopier or a car. . . ."[57]

E-government initiatives can have three primary benefits—increased access to information about government programs and policies, better service delivery to citizens and businesses, and greater citizen involvement in government decisionmaking. In some countries, simply the increased transparency associated with readily available, but static, information about the identities of responsible government officials, about how to contact them, or about the proper procedures for a given service, is a potentially large change. For many governments, the holy grail of e-government is Internet-based transactions that save money and allow citizens and businesses easy, anytime, anywhere service. To achieve this sort of "one-stop shop," historically "stove-pipe" government agencies must coordinate their activities because "transformation comes not from moving services online, but from redesigning the organization and processes to put the citizen at the center, integrating across agencies to simplify interaction, reduce cost and improve service."[58] Last, IT has the potential to enhance democracy by allowing citizens to participate in debates as they happen, overcoming boundaries of geography and giving many people and organizations access to information once restricted to the powerful few. We do not examine in depth another advantage of technology from the point of view of some governments—an increased ability to monitor the citizenry.

As with the effect of IT on politics in Asian countries, the picture when looking at top-down e-government is quite varied in Asia. Some countries are e-government leaders where others have but simple websites. Overall, IT's "wonderful potential has been hardly used in most Asia-Pacific countries" for e-government.[59] Unlike with the case of internal politics, IT has not lead to dramatic changes in the *substance* of government in any country. In some countries, however, changes in the form of government have been so substantial that they are approaching changes in substance. In others, such as China, e-government could lead to actual changes in governance

---

[57]Wescott (2001, p. 3).

[58]Accenture (2002).

[59] Wescott (2001, p. 6).

in the future by disguising government reform under the cover of hardware and software.

The Asian governments that routinely place within the top ten in the world for e-government according to various survey groups include Australia, Singapore, Hong Kong, New Zealand, and Taiwan (see

Table 2.3

### Rankings of e-Government

| | Accenture[a] | | United Nations[b] | | | World Markets/Brown[c] | |
|---|---|---|---|---|---|---|---|
| | Rank (of 23) | Category (of 4) | Rank (of 144) | Score (3.25 Is Top) | E-government Capacity (of four levels) | Rank (of 196) | Percent |
| Australia | 4 | Visionary challenger | 2 | 2.60 | High | 3 | 50.7 |
| China | | | 93 | 1.04 | Minimal | 83 | 30.2 |
| Hong Kong | 8 | Visionary challenger | | | | | |
| India | | | 79 | 1.29 | Minimal | 69 | 31.8 |
| Indonesia | | | 75 | 1.34 | Minimal | | |
| Japan | 17 | Emerging performer | 27 | 2.12 | High | 38 | 34.9 |
| South Korea | | | 15 | 2.30 | High | 47 | 33.4 |
| Malaysia | 19 | Platform builder | | | | 16 | 39.0 |
| New Zealand | 14 | Emerging performer | 3 | 2.59 | High | 26 | 36.8 |
| Philippines | | | 68 | 1.44 | Minimal | 52 | 32.8 |
| Singapore | 2 | Innovative leader | 4 | 2.58 | High | 8 | 43.4 |
| Taiwan | | | | | | 2 | 52.5 |
| Thailand | | | 103 | .94 | Deficient | 71 | 30.8 |
| Vietnam | | | 90 | 1.10 | Minimal | 53 | 32.8 |

SOURCES: [a]Accenture (2002). This study looked only at Internet-based e-government. [b]United Nations (2002). This survey looked solely at the web presence of U.N. member states at the national level. [c]World Markets Research Centre (2001). This survey looked only at websites.

Table 2.3).[60] Others are devoting significant amounts of time and resources to e-government but have not reached a level of global sophistication; those include Thailand, the Philippines, and Malaysia.
Countries such as India and China have remarkable pockets of innovation in local polities but are in the early stages overall. North
Korea, Myanmar, Vietnam, and Indonesia have not developed robust
e-government programs.

## One-Party Dominant States

**Singapore.** Of the one-party dominant nations in Asia, the city-state
of Singapore is undoubtedly the most advanced in e-government.
Singapore routinely ranks among the top three in the world for its e-
government program. It began earlier and advanced more rapidly
than most other Asian countries. A program to train government
workers in information technology began in 1981.[61] The year 1995
was the transitional year in which the government went from virtual
ignorance of the Internet to having all of the 36 government agencies
and ministries online.[62] Now all bureaucrats in Singapore communicate by e-mail. At the same time, Internet penetration among the
population increased rapidly, now exceeding 50 percent, and the
government has placed Internet kiosks in community centers, making online service delivery to most citizens a viable option.[63] All
ministries have a web presence, coordinated through a central portal. And unlike many other governments in Asia and elsewhere,
where users must eventually print out information and consummate
transactions manually, Singapore allows many transactions to be
started and completed online, from renewing a driver's license to en-
rolling in school. By October 2001, according to the government,
1,700 out of 2,600 total public services offered were available online,
and government plans project that all citizen and business transac-

---

[60]It is important to note what the surveys are actually measuring. Most judge only
government websites, as opposed to other delivery methods. Most are focused on
services as opposed to "e-democracy" efforts.

[61]International Telecommunications Union (2001, p. 30).

[62]See Quah and Hai (2002). Also see Kalathil and Boas (2002).

[63]Access prices in Singapore are lower than in many other countries. See International Telecommunications Union (2001, p. 20).

tions with the government will be available online in 2003.[64] Singapore was one of the first countries to pass legislation to legally recognize the use of electronic signatures.

E-Citizen, www.ecitizen.gov.sg, among other services, allows users to apply for a birth certificate, a government job, maternity leave, or government housing online. The portal is organized around online "towns" that reflect the needs of citizens rather than lines of government bureaucracy. "Business Town" features a one-stop licensing center for some small businesses, allowing application to all necessary government agencies at one time, cutting processing time from six to eight weeks down to two.[65] "Family Town" offers such options as "find a soulmate," "get married," and "care for your child." "Sports Town" allows citizens to book tickets to sporting events as well as calculate their fitness quotient. Housing Town, Transportation Town, and Health Town are other destinations.[66] Singapore has brought technology to the courts as well. Registered users can file small claims online at www.smallclaims.gov.sg. Also, in one of the few e-government programs to use mobile phones in Asia, the Supreme Court recently launched an SMS service to alert citizens to the times and dates of trials.[67] Not surprisingly, efforts to include citizen input in government policies have not been emphasized in Singapore.

**China.** Compared to Singapore, China's e-government is rudimentary overall. Conditions in some local areas, however, have allowed progressive e-government initiatives to flourish.[68] The case of China is also important as it raises the question of whether technological reform can enable real political reform. Rhetoric about e-government in China is certainly thick. The government declared 1999 to be "Government Online" year, requiring certain percentages of government offices to establish websites. Now there are close to 10,000 ".gov.cn" cites in China,[69] but the vast majority of government

---

[64]"E-government" (2002, p. 2).

[65]See "E-government" (2002, p. 5).

[66]For more on E-Citizen, see Holmes (2001, p. 24).

[67]Accenture (2002, p. 37).

[68]For more on China's e-government initiatives, see Zhang and Woesler (2002).

[69]According to China's official statistics, as of January 2003. See www.cnnic.net.cn.

websites still simply post basic, often outdated, information or "brochure-ware," to attract foreign investment and do not deliver information or services that benefit citizens or businesses. Efforts to computerize and harmonize internal government workings also proceed, but at a slow pace. The central government is constructing a series of Intranets for tax, banking, agriculture, and other systems, that are to link local bureaus throughout the country to the center. These now 20 "Golden Projects" are designed to improve Beijing's control over activities in the provinces. "Golden Tax" and "Golden Customs" are already paying dividends, with tariff payments in 2000 up by 22.8 percent.[70]

Some ministries in China are moving quickly down the e-government path. Already businesses can use the Customs Administration website to find out what duties they will owe on certain goods, and the Ministry of Agriculture's intranet permits documents to be approved and reviewed online, as well as the more efficient collection of farming data.[71]    The Ministry of Foreign Trade's robust website reportedly gets 720,000 hits per day.[72]    Also, the People's Bank of China is issuing "smart cards" with financial histories to businesses. To get a loan, officers of the company must produce the smart card. The central government is also actively using IT for propaganda delivery. It has invested millions of dollars in establishing mega news portals that relay the Communist Party line on current events. As of May 2001, there were 12 such government-sponsored sites.[73]

*Provincial and Local Examples.* The real energy for e-government in China, however, is at the provincial and local level where some Chinese officials are embracing e-government. Especially in the coastal and wealthier cities, some progressive officials have focused on e-government improvements, even those that involve greater citizen input to government decisions. According to a survey by Fudan Uni-

---

[70]Zhang (2002, p. 163); see also Cartledge and Lovelock (1999) and Kalathil and Boas (2003).

[71]Kalathil and Boas (2003).

[72]Zhang (2002, p. 177).

[73]Zhang (2002, p. 168).

versity, 28.4 percent of "ordinary people" surveyed in ten large Chinese cities had visited a municipal government website.[74]

The city of Beijing has a unified portal that links 123 agencies and districts in the city. In 2000, in a decision uncharacteristic of a communist bureaucracy, the municipal government asked outside experts to independently rate the quality of its websites. Criteria included clarity and timeliness of posted information, and other cities were used as comparisons. Poor performance motivated subsequent website improvements. In addition, the city is enabling better citizen communication with government. The website solicits e-mail suggestions from citizens or invites them to "criticize work you're dissatisfied with."[75] Beijing officials have anecdotal evidence that the mayor's office and city departments have responded promptly to citizen complaints forwarded through e-mail about problems such as pot holes.[76] In the high-tech zone of Beijing, the Zhongguamen Science Park, home to over 6,000 companies, has streamlined its registration process. Instead of a minimum of 15 visits to various offices, which took at least 15 days, new companies can register with the e-park entirely online, no matter where they are located, and can track which official is reviewing their documents. The application process now takes three days. The monthly reporting of commercial data that e-Park companies must do is also now entirely online.[77]

Shanghai is perhaps the city in China most vocal about its e-government progress. More than other cities, Shanghai appears to want to use e-government to reorganize and reform the city bureaucracy. As the Vice-Mayor put it in a recent speech, e-government should be used to "break the traditional organization border of the administrative organs, re-organize the business process according to the needs of the public and enterprises, pay more attention to providing the society with wide, effective and personal services."[78] The main Shanghai portal, www.shanghai.com, gets 100,000 hits a day, and a "mayor box" solicits opinions from the public. One part of Shang-

---

[74]Jiang (forthcoming).

[75]Wescott (2001, p. 14).

[76]Interviews with Beijing government officials, February 2001.

[77]See www1.worldbank.org/publicsector/egov/zhongguancun_cs.htm.

[78]Speech by Yan (2002).

hai's effort is focused on harmonizing the government's social service programs. Officials are instituting a system of smart cards for all Shanghai citizens that identify citizens and contain their medical records and information about their health insurance, unemployment benefits, workers compensation, and pension so that records about individual citizens are portable and easily shared among different government bureaus dealing with citizens' social welfare. This system, with an abundance of personal information in government databases, will, of course, also give Shanghai more control over its citizens.

Finally, the Communist Party Secretary of Nanhai, a small city of one million in the south of China, is a true believer in information technology. Nanhai boasts an online metals exchange, an agricultural export site, and a mayor's mailbox. In addition, all schools are wired to each other, and there is an online medical clinic where people can ask medical personnel for advice. An e-procurement system posts bid solicitation but does not allow online bidding. A legal case tracking system called "e-court" allows parties to track the status of any case in the court system through the web. And the central website, www.nanhai.gov.cn, provides a detailed overview of the government's workings.

*Implications.* These projects, of course, are not representative. Most local governments in China are concentrating on the very first steps—computerizing government processes, establishing intranets, and posting generic information. But these unusual initiatives raise an important question—are these reforms in the name of technology masking true reform of the Communist bureaucracy? It is true that "many Party cadres and others genuinely desire some degree of political reform. . . . These officials see informatization as a force breaking down dusty hierarchies within the state structure and fostering new organizations in a middle layer between state and society."[79]    Forward-thinking officials hope to harness the momentum from the excitement over IT in China to push through needed reforms, where past efforts have failed. This is an urgent but extremely difficult undertaking. Chinese bureaucracy is huge, complicated, opaque, and multilayered. Its fragmented, overlapping

---

[79]Kalathil and Boas (2003).

lines of authority travel both vertically and horizontally, and it is still heavily dependent on paper documents with official stamps. The Communist Party itself has an independent but parallel structure.

That many government offices now post their hours, their responsibilities, the names of officials in charge, and the requirements and procedures for getting certain licenses, permits, and approvals is in itself a significant step. In the Fudan University study, ordinary people and government workers both chose the ability of people to get "political information" as the way e-government will most improve government, even over greater government "efficiency."[80] They also responded that more "responsible" government should be the top priority for government reform.

In addition to greater transparency, the possibility that e-government will enable greater citizen input into government decisionmaking is potentially potent. At the national level, a few experiments have invited citizen input into central government decisionmaking. In 2002, cell phone users were invited to send text messages to the annual meeting of the National People's Congress, China's legislature. Officials said the move was designed to create a "new channel to become familiar with public opinion," and in the first day of the session, over 2,000 messages were logged.[81] It is unclear the degree to which the legislators, not elected by the populace, were exposed to the messages and what their effect was. Also, according to an account by a state news agency, when the tenth Five Year Plan was being drafted, over 10,000 suggestions were sent via e-mail to official websites, and China's State Planning Commission took up 300 of them.[82] At this stage, the future import of these few forays by the national government into techno-democracy is difficult to gauge. They could represent reform in the disguise of technology—a palatable way of increasing the voice of the people by bureaucrats who understand that the Party must change. More likely, they are show pieces designed to make the regime seem more modern but not to foster real change. In either case, if these initiatives are successful at increasing the citizenry's belief that they are being represented, or

---

[80]Jiang (forthcoming).

[81]"Reach China's Politicians via SMS" (2002).

[82]"Internet: Bliss and Pain to the Chinese" (2002).

even incorporating their actual input, without threatening the regime's power, perhaps they will be expanded.

At the local level, some efforts at citizen involvement may be more genuine. As noted above, many local governments now have e-mail boxes and there is anecdotal evidence that at least some inquiries are read and responded to. Hangzhou, a smaller coastal city, has gone further. There the government has invited to meetings citizens who sent particularly thoughtful suggestions by e-mail. The mayor's office also conducted an online poll about whether firecrackers should be allowed during Spring Festival. Citizen voting, no matter how trivial the issue, is a notable occurrence in China.

In the long run, e-government in China has the potential to make a difference to governance. Citizen expectations of transparency and participation may ultimately be hard to reverse, and pressure could build for deeper changes. It is difficult at this early stage to predict whether or when e-government will have a tangible political effect.

**Hong Kong.** Now also part of China, Hong Kong has been pursuing an advanced e-government program distinguished by its extremely close partnership with the private sector. The main government portal is entirely financed and maintained by ESD Services Limited, which charges user fees and permits some private sector advertising. By October 2001, the site www.esd.gov.hk had attracted 18 million visitors and had concluded over 950,000 transactions.[83] Users can apply for birth certificates, register to vote, sign up for a marriage license, and download legislative proposals, among a variety of other services. These services are available through any computer with Internet access and are also offered on specially designed kiosks installed throughout the city. E-procurement is also a focus, with the government aiming to carry out 80 percent of government tenders online by the end of 2003. In March 2002, the Hong Kong government announced that it would issue new "smart cards" to all residents by 2003 that will contain a digital thumbprint and photo of the holder. Many have expressed concern about possible identity theft by hackers.[84]

---

[83]Accenture (2002, p. 55).

[84]Yu (2002).

**Others.** As for other one-party dominant states in Asia, Malaysia has made headway in a few discrete areas of e-government, such as Web-enabled bill payment systems for citizens.[85] It is also initiating a program called "MyKad," an identity card that functions as a driver's license and will also hold "eCash." The government estimates that 20 million Malaysians will hold the card by 2007.[86] Such cards may be designed to increase the government's ability to monitor citizen activity. Despite its uneven progress, given the regime's focus on technology and technology education for its citizens, Malaysia could advance quickly. In contrast, e-government in North Korea and Myanmar consists now and in the foreseeable future of a few government websites with propaganda for tourists and the media. No relevant information or services are available for citizens.

## Liberal Democracies

**Australia.** The liberal democracies of Asia are also implementing e-government to varying degrees. Along with Singapore, Australia also consistently ranks among the most advanced e-government leaders in the world. Its sophisticated e-government program delivers over 100 government services to citizens and businesses online. Unlike most countries, Australia also keeps close track of its progress on e-government at the national level, with all government departments regularly reporting on their progress against standard measures.[87] The National Office for the Information Economy (NOIE) coordinates all government initiatives for e-government and the information economy.[88] A single portal, www.australia.gov.au, connects visitors to all government web pages, and progress toward a full e-procurement system is well under way. The "Business Entry Point," www.business.gov.au, allows businesses to conduct transactions not only with the national government but with state and local entities as well. Such cross-governmental coordination is still very rare in e-government schemes. Seventy five percent of all income tax forms

---

[85]See Accenture (2002, p. 62).

[86]Accenture (2002, p. 35).

[87]Accenture (2002, p. 13).

[88]www.noie.gov.au.

are filled electronically through the tax office website.[89]  Australian job seekers can submit their resumes online on a national job database, www.jobsearch.gov.au, on which Australian companies post vacancies.  Another of its flagship programs is the online federal court, www.fedcourt.gov.au, which allows litigants to submit documents electronically.[90]  The Human Rights and Equal Opportunity Commission, www.hreoc.gov.au, allows for online filing of discrimination complaints.  A recent survey showed that one in four Australians had visited a government site during July 2001.[91]

But most unique in Asia is Australia's progress in "e-democracy."  At both the national and local levels, Australia has found innovative ways to use IT to involve citizens in government debates and decisionmaking.  The Australian Senate, for example, "is one of the few parliamentary chambers in the world to grant electronic petitions the same status as those signed by hand.  The Senate also accepts electronic submissions to committee deliberations."[92]  The NOIE noted in a March 2002 statement that "Australia's position as a world leader in eGovernment continues to be reflected in progress regarding e-democracy."[93]

Australia's state of Queensland has published an "E-Democracy Policy Framework," which promises that by late 2002, the government will post issues on its website and solicit citizen feedback, provide online access to documents such as policy papers and draft bills; broadcast Parliamentary debates online, and develop a system to accept petitions to the Queensland Parliament online.  A large team of government officials is dedicated to implementing this plan, coordinated by the specially designated "E-Democracy Unit."  The parliament of another state, Victoria, is actively seeking to grow its e-democracy programs from the efforts at increasing transparency to those that allow citizen interaction.[94]  In Brisbane, citizens can regis-

---

[89]Holmes (2001).

[90]Accenture (2002).

[91]Accenture (2002, p. 38).

[92]Gibson and Ward (2002, p. 4).

[93]National Office for the Information Economy (2002).

[94]www.vic.gov.au.  More about the e-democracy inquiry of Victoria's parliament can be found at www.parliament.vic.gov.au/sarc/Current%20Inquires.htm.

ter to participate in the "Your City Your Say" online mediated discussions on subjects that change weekly.[95]

**New Zealand.** New Zealand is on the brink of launching a number of ambitious e-government programs, from a unified government portal to complete online services. The government has constructed a comprehensive website devoted to explaining what e-government is and where the implementation stands from month to month. New Zealand is distinguishing itself by working closely with its citizens to build the applications that are most desired.[96]

**South Korea.** South Korea has a well-developed e-government structure, with a one-stop portal, www.egov.go.kr, and many online services available to businesses and citizens. One of the focuses of the Korean e-government initiative has been to fight corruption. For example, a key benefit of the National Tax Service's Tax Integrated System, www.nta.go.kr, is that the computerization and analyses of citizen tax information makes it more difficult for tax officials to unfairly single out citizens for audits. It also makes the once millions of face-to-face meetings with tax officials unnecessary, reducing opportunities for official mischief.[97] An electronic procurement system confers similar advantages. Perhaps the most well-known of Korea's anticorruption initiatives is the "Online Procedures Enhancement for Civil Applications," or "OPEN" project in the capital city of Seoul, www.open.metro.seoul.kr. Corruption in the municipal government became a major problem as Seoul grew rapidly in the 1990s. City officials computerized those services that citizens, in a survey, had chosen as the most inconvenient or subject to irregularities. These services are now available via the Internet where the procedures are posted, department and staff in charge listed, and phone numbers given. Applicants can monitor which official is reviewing their application and where it is in the process. A survey indicated that 84 percent of citizens who used OPEN thought that it had increased transparency.[98] Newly elected President Roh solicited recommendations for his cabinet online, in an early sign of his interest.

---

[95]Holmes (2001, p. 275).

[96]See http://www.e-government.govt.nz/ for more on New Zealand's e-government.

[97]Wescott (2001, p. 13).

[98]See World Bank (2002c). See also Park (n.d.).

**Taiwan.** The E-Taiwan Project is to make Taiwan "fully digital" by 2008, at a projected cost of over $1 billion, which includes broadband access for six million households in addition to ambitious e-government plans. Interestingly, Taiwan is also taking a page from the NGO handbook and using the Internet in its effort to bolster its diplomatic status in the international community. In May 2002, the Ministry of Foreign Affairs launched an Internet letter campaign to promote its bid to join the World Health Organization (WHO) as an observer, asking its citizens to write to the WHO Director General.[99] Former President Lee Tung-hui also recently launched a pro-independence Internet radio station designed to influence the local and international debate surrounding Taiwan's status in relation to the People's Republic of China.[100]

**India.** India presents a situation somewhat similar to that of China. At the national level, India has not made e-government a priority. Neither computerization of services, nor bureaucratic integration, nor efforts to use IT to enhance citizen participation are very far along. But a few states in India have conducted bold experiments in e-government, many of which have made an appreciable difference in their citizens' lives. In Andhra Pradesh, for example, which has pioneered many innovative e-government applications, the Computer-aided Administration of Registration Department (CARD) system has reformed a once corrupt, opaque, and inefficient system of land registration. When a parcel of land changes hands in India, the details must be recorded and fees paid to the government—1.2 million deeds are registered each year in the state. The procedure once involved several complicated steps, offered opportunities for unofficial brokers to profit, and took a week's time to complete. CARD now operates with much greater transparency at computerized counters in over 200 locations in the state and registering a deed takes an hour.[101]

In 2000, the award-winning "Gyandoot" program established an Intranet that links hundreds of villages in Madhya Pradesh, a very poor,

---

[99]Wu (2002).

[100]"Vice-President, former President Attend pro-Taiwan Internet Radio Launch" (2002).

[101]See World Bank (2002b). See also Satyanarayana (2002).

rural state.  At kiosks distributed around the state, with the assistance of attendants, farmers can check market prices of agricultural products themselves, thus avoiding profiteering middlemen.  Among other services, villagers can also lodge complaints with the government and much more easily obtain land title documents that they need every season to obtain bank loans.  During the project's first 11 months, the 31 Gyandoot kiosks were used nearly 55,000 times.[102] Despite these and many other progressive projects that can be found throughout India, most government functions, in most places, remain inefficient and opaque.

**Japan.**  Just as IT has had little effect on Japan's internal politics, Japan's steps into the e-government realm have been very limited thus far.  In fact, use of government services online actually *decreased* from 2001 to 2002.[103]  Given its status as a major producer and user of IT products in Asia, and its relative wealth, this is surprising.  Explanations include the terrible financial posture of the government and perhaps the lack of enthusiasm on the part of the entrenched ruling LDP for increased transparency for government operations.

The January 2001 IT blueprint for the country, the *eJapan Strategy*, promises a more aggressive push for e-government, at the local and national levels, in the future.  The government plans to have all administrative services available online by the end of 2003.[104]  One of the most innovative programs is Prime Minister Junichiro Koizumi's e-mail newsletter.  In its first month, two million citizens subscribed to the weekly "magazine" that describes government goings-on from the Prime Minister's point of view—a useful political tool.  The leading opposition party, Minshuto, has followed Koizumi's lead and is now soliciting policy proposals from voters on the Internet.  Among other advanced programs is a site that allows businesses to review open bids for government services, www.jetro.go.jp, and a well-organized employment site that brings together open positions with job seekers.  The Ministry of Justice allows users to search bills online at www.moj.go.jp.  Also, the Ministry of Land, Infrastructure and Transport, www.ochi.mlit.go.jp, offers an interactive land title

---

[102]See World Bank (2002a).  See also Holmes (2001, p. 26).

[103]"Asia-Pacific Shows High Use of Gov't Online Services" (2002).

[104]See Nakagawa (2002).

search.[105] Japan's real e-government potential lies in SMS. With cell phones so pervasive, and texting so popular, Japan could offer a wealth of services and information to citizens via their phones. To date, only some traffic and postal information has been available.

**Philippines.** Although making relatively minor strides in e-government overall, the Philippines has a number of worthwhile efforts under way focused, as is South Korea, on reducing corruption.[106] The national budget system is remarkably transparent, for example, with all accounts payable for all agencies, and amounts released to vendors all posted online so that contractors can check bureaucrats' statements against the official books.[107] The Bureau of Customs has developed electronic systems for processing customs clearance documents and making payments. The time for reconciling customs payments has gone from four months to a few days.[108] The bureau also launched three mobile-phone-based services in February 2002 to streamline the payment of duties and allow surfing of the bureau website via cell phone.[109]

**Thailand.** The Thai government wants to develop a robust e-government program—it is passing the necessary enabling legislation, developing a policy framework, and designating the personnel to implement the plan.[110] But it is wrestling with a number of hurdles, including the lack of IT access in rural areas where most of the population lives, lack of literacy in English/lack of Thai content, incompatible systems in different parts of the government, and inadequate training of officials.[111] The best progress seems to be in wiring schools and offering free Internet access through the SchoolNet program. As of January 2002, over 4,200 schools were online. Other pilot projects in e-customs and e-voting are also under way.

---

[105]Accenture (2002, pp. 60–61).

[106]For a comprehensive study of Philippine e-Government, see Lallana et al. (2002).

[107]Wescott (2001, p. 13).

[108]Wescott (2001, p. 16).

[109]Lallana et al. (2002).

[110]See Koanantakool (2002).

[111]Amin (2001).

## Analysis and Future Trends

As with the case for bottom-up initiatives in internal politics, the effect of IT on government does not correlate to government type. As a group, the liberal democracies tend to have pursued e-government to a greater degree, but not categorically—India is much less advanced than Singapore. The priorities of governments do appear, not surprisingly, in what e-government applications they chose to emphasize. Australia concentrates on e-democracy, for example, whereas India's programs focus on development.

E-government in some Asian countries is providing concrete dividends to some individual citizens and businesses: They waste less time with routine government interactions, they pay fewer bribes, they are better informed about government policies, and they can comment on them no matter how far away they live. Government in Singapore and Hong Kong is faster and easier to negotiate; government in South Korea is less corrupt; government in Australia and New Zealand is more democratic, partly because of technology. The critical question is whether these incremental changes will amount to fundamental alterations in the way governments govern or citizens and government relate to one another, that is, determining when, as Lawrence Lessig puts it, a "difference in degree . . . ripens into a difference in kind."[112] As Joseph Nye has said, "The effects on central governments of the . . . information revolution are still in their early stages."[113]

Because e-government is implemented so differently in various Asian countries, there are few sweeping generalities to be made about its future substantive progression. In most countries, e-government will likely continue to develop on its current course, although e-government plans are always vulnerable to changes in leadership. Singapore will continue to push the envelope of progressive initiatives that make government seamless, ease the lives of citizens and businesses, but still leave the ruling party in control. Transparent, largely accountable and responsive governments, such as Australia and New Zealand, will continue to involve citizens in the

---

[112]Lessig (1999, p. 21).

[113]Nye (1999, p. 11).

business of government, perhaps to the point of changing the way policies are formed. South Korea's government will become more efficient and transparent as the focus on corruption continues. Japan may make a leap toward bolder programs, but the bureaucracy will fight any initiatives that promise real transparency and responsiveness. India's entrepreneurial local officials will sustain their pursuit of exciting, but relatively small, programs. There is a chance that e-government will usher in more significant government reform in China, a country where technology has sometimes been a window of clarity in an otherwise opaque, corrupt, and unresponsive system.

In the future, governments will follow the private sector in testing new delivery mechanisms for e-government, such as SMS. Also, the government and the private sector will grow more intertwined as technology companies look for new markets and governments realize that they need private sector expertise to succeed. This partnership will raise difficult questions of cost allocation, data ownership, and privacy. Asian countries will continue to grapple with the current obstacles to e-government—security concerns, bureaucracies resistant to change, lack of consistent leadership, lack of enabling legislation, lack of computer skills among government workers, low literacy, low technology penetration, and budget constraints.

## CONCLUSION

The effect of the information revolution on politics and governance in Asia presents a varied picture, one not easily organized by government type. IT has been responsible for political change in liberal democracies and one-party dominant states alike. Likewise, different governments from across the ideological spectrum have used and ignored the possibilities of IT for governance.

Three trajectories will determine the future role of IT on politics in Asian countries. First, IT's effect will reflect the degree of future technology penetration in a given population and what population segments benefit. Second, the political momentum within a polity for political stasis or change will define those who might seek to harness IT. Last, the ability and desire of the government to control challenges to its authority will influence whether IT-enabled political movements do cause lasting shifts. In any political transitions that do occur in any wired country in Asia, IT will no doubt play a large role.  Moreover, NGOs will continue to exploit its potential to exert domestic and international pressure for policy change.  Finally, e-government has the potential to usher in significant change in the relationship between government and citizens, but most such shifts will be gradual.

# BIBLIOGRAPHY

Accenture, "eGovernment Leadership—Realizing the Vision," Thailand, April 2002, available at www.acenture.com as of September 2002.

Amin, Magdi, "Accelerating E-readiness in Thailand: A Case Study," paper presented at the Asian Development Forum, June 14, 2001.

Ang, Audra, "Beijing Closes Internet Cafes After Fatal Fire Amid Nationwide Crackdown on Cyber Bars," *Associated Press*, June 17, 2002.

Applied Materials annual financial reports, filed with the U.S. Securities Exchange Commission.

Arquilla, John, and David Ronfeldt, *In Athena's Camp: Preparing for Conflict in the Information Age*, Santa Monica, Calif.: RAND MR-880-OSD/RC, 1997.

Arquilla, John, and David Ronfeldt, *The Advent of Netwar*, Santa Monica, Calif.: RAND MR-789-OSD, 1996.

*Asia Pacific Adds 104 Million Mobile Subscribers in 2002*, February 28, 2003, available at www.cellular-news.com as of March 2003.

"Asia-Pacific Shows High Use of Gov't Online Services," *Business World*, November 12, 2002.

Bagalwis, Jennifer E., "Philippines: How Technology Helped Kick Out a President," *Computerworld (Philippines)*, January 29, 2001.

Bariuad, Arturo, "Phone Text Messages Woo Filipino Voters," *The Straits Times (Singapore)*, February 25, 2001.

BBC News, "Hong Kong Bans Overseas Gambling," May 31, 2002.

Cartledge, S., and P. Lovelock, "Special Subject: E-China," *China Economic Quarterly*, 1999.

Chase, Michael, and James Mulvenon, *You've Got Dissent! Chinese Dissident Use of the Internet and Beijing's Counter-Strategies*, Santa Monica, Calif.: RAND MR-1543, 2002.

Chin, J., "Malaysiakini and its Impact on Journalism and Politics in Malaysia," *Internet Political Economy Forum*, "Internet and Development in Asia," Singapore, September 14–15, 2001.

Choi, Seon-Kyou, Myeong-Ho Lee, and Gyu-Hwa Chang, *Competition in Korean Mobile Telecommunications Market: Business Strategy and Regulatory Environment*, Taejon, South Korea: Information and Communications University, December 2000.

Chon, Shi-yong, "Disclosure of Candidates' Criminal Records Expected to Sway Close Contests," *The Korea Herald*, April 8, 2000.

CS First Boston, *2002 Asia Telecoms Sector Strategy*, Hong Kong: CS First Boston, November 26, 2001.

Dang, Hoang-Giang, "Internet in Vietnam: From a Laborious Birth into an Uncertain Future," *Informatik Forum*, Wein, Germany, January 1999, available at www.fgi.at/if as of April 2003.

Demick, Barbara, "'Netizens' Crusade Buoys New South Korean Leader," *Los Angeles Times*, February 10, 2003.

"Digital Divide," *Bangkok Post*, August 15, 2001.

"DoCoMo Director: Cell Phone Service Growth Too Slow," *Nikkei Financial Daily*, June 4, 2002.

Eder, Ederic Penaflor, "People Power Underscored Issues of New Media Access," *Philippine Journalism Review*, March 2001, pp. 23–24, available at www.cmfr.com.ph as of September 2002.

"E-government," *IDA Singapore*, Issue 5, January 2002, p. 2, available at www.itu.int/asean2001/reports/material/SGP%20CS.pdf as of July 2002.

Expedia first-quarter 2002 financial report (10-K form), filed with the U.S. Securities Exchange Commission.

Federal Communications Commission report, February 2002, cited in "Broadband Keeps Users Glued To Computer," *San Francisco Chronicle*, June 24, 2002, p. E3.

Foster, William, and Seymour E. Goodman, *The Diffusion of the Internet in China*, Stanford, Calif.: Center for International Security and Cooperation, November 2000.

Gibson, Rachel, and Stephen J. Ward, "Virtual Campaigning: Australian Parties and the Impact of the Internet," *Australian Journal of Political Science*, Vol. 37, No. 1, March 2002.

Global Sources annual financial reports, filed with the U.S. Securities Exchange Commission.

"Govt, LDP May OK Internet Campaigns," *The Daily Yomiuri*, January 7, 2002.

Guest, Robert, "Fewer Buffaloes, Livelier Democracy," *The Economist*, November 10, 2001.

Guo, Liang, "The Internet: China's Window to the World," YaleGlobal, November 18, 2002, available at yaleglobal.yale.edu/display.article?id=362&page=1, as of February 2003.

Guo, Liang, and Bu Wei, *Hulianwang shiyong zhuangkuang ji yingxiang de diaocha baogao* (Survey Report on Internet Usage and Impact), Beijing: Chinese Academy of Social Sciences, April 2001; Chinese version available at www.chinace.org/ce/itre/ as of September 2002.

Gupta, Sunil, *Industry Overview: Asia Pacific Handsets: Design and Scale Are Key*, Morgan Stanley, February 25, 2003.

Gutmann, Ethan, "Who Lost China's Internet," *The Weekly Standard*, February 25, 2002.

Hachigian, Nina, "China's Cyber-Strategy," *Foreign Affairs*, Vol. 80, No. 2, March/April 2001, pp. 118–133.

Hachigian, Nina, "The Internet and Power in One-Party East Asian States," *The Washington Quarterly*, Vol. 25, No. 3, Summer 2002, pp. 41–58.

Hartford, Kathleen, "Cyberspace with Chinese Characteristics," *Current History*, Vol. 99, No. 638, 2000.

Harwit, Eric, and Duncan Clark, "Shaping the Internet in China: Evolution of Political Control over Network Infrastructure and Content," *Asian Survey*, Vol. 41, No. 3, 2001.

Hill, David T., "East Timor and the Internet: Global Political Leverage in/on Indonesia," *Indonesia (Cornell University)*, No. 73, April 2002, p. 25.

Hill, Kevin A., and John E. Hughes, *Cyberpolitics*, Oxford, England: Rowman & Littlefield Publishers, Inc., 1998, p. 2.

Holmes, Douglas, *E.Gov: E-business Strategies for Government*, Nicholas Brealey Publishing, London, 2001, p. 24.

How, Tan Tarn, "Sintercom Founder Fades Out of Cyberspace," *The Straits Times (Singapore)*, August 22, 2001.

Hua, Vanessa, "India's Ties to Bay Area Still Strong," *San Francisco Chronicle*, June 10, 2002.

Hung, Faith, "Chartered Names New Chief Executive," *Electronics Business News*, June 25, 2002.

"Information on Listed Companies," available at www.hkgem.com/root/e_default.asp as of June 2002.

International Data Corp., *The Internet Market in Asia Pacific 1998–2004*, Hong Kong: IDC, July 2000.

International Data Corp., *Early Trends of the IP-VPN Market in Asia/Pacific*, Hong Kong: IDC, March 2001.

International Data Corp., "CRM Market in Asia Pacific," IDC press release, Hong Kong, January 21, 2002a, and April 22, 2002b.

International Data Corp., "eGovernment Emerges As Key Priority for Asia's Governments," IDC press release, Hong Kong, February 11, 2002c.

International Data Corp., "World Server Market Statistics," IDC press release, Hong Kong, February 25, 2002d.

International Data Corp., "World PC Market Statistics," IDC press release, Hong Kong, April 23, 2002e.

International Data Corp., "CRM Market in Japan," IDC press release, Hong Kong, May 9, 2002f.

International Monetary Fund, *World Economic Outlook*, Washington, D.C., 2002.

International Telecommunications Union (ITU), "The e-City: Singapore Internet Case Study," 2001, p. 30, available at www.itu.int/asean2001/reports/material/SGP%20CS.pdf, as of July 2002.

"Internet Activism in Asia," 2002, available at journalism.uts.edu.au/subjects/oj1/oj1_a2002/internetactivisminasia/india1.html as of February 2003.

"Internet: Bliss and Pain to the Chinese," *Xinhuanet*, June 28, 2002.

James, Geoffrey, "Out of Their Minds: Pundits Can't Stop Hyping the Business Opportunities of Artificial Intelligence," *Red Herring*, August 2002.

Jiang, Changjian, *An Investigative Report on Social Base of Electronic Public Services in Ten Cities of China*, San Francisco, Calif.: Asia Foundation, forthcoming.

J.P. Morgan, *China Telecoms: Regulatory Risk and Long-Term Returns in Mobile and Fixed Line Businesses*, Hong Kong: J. P. Morgan, May 5, 2001.

Kalathil, Shanthi, "Chinese Media and the Information Revolution," *Harvard Asia Quarterly*, Winter 2002.

Kalathil, Shanthi, and Taylor C. Boas, *Open Networks, Closed Regimes: The Impact of the Internet on Authoritarian Rule*, Washington, D.C.: Carnegie Endowment for International Peace, 2003.

Kedzie, Christopher, *Dictator's Dilemma,* Santa Monica, Calif.: RAND MR-678.0-RC, 1996.

Koanantakool, Thaweesak, "The Development of ICT in Thailand," presentation to APRICOT March 5, 2002, available at www.nectec. or.th/users/htk/publish/a2002.ppt as of September 2002.

Lallana, Emmanuel, Patricia Pascual, and Edwin Soriano, "e-Government in the Philippines: Benchmarking Against Global Practices," *Digital Philippines,* April 2002.

Lee, Ho-chul, "North Korea's Information Technology Revolution" in *The Korean Peninsula in the 21st Century: Prospects for Stability and Cooperation,* Symposium volume, Washington, D.C.: Korean Economic Institute, 2000, pp. 25–60.

Lessig, Lawrence, *Code and Other Laws of Cyberspace,* Basic Books, New York, 1999, p. 21.

Lynch, Daniel, *After the Propaganda State: Media, Politics and "Thought Work" in Reformed China,* Stanford, Calif.: Stanford University Press, 1999.

Marcus, David L., "Indonesia Revolt Was Net Driven," *The Boston Globe,* May 23, 1998.

Market Intelligence Center press release, "Taiwanese Notebook PC Output in 2H2002," May 6, 2002, available at mic.iii.org.tw/english as of June 2002.

"MDP Begins Internet Voting for Presidential Primary," *The Korea Herald,* April 19, 2002, available at www.koreaherald.co.kr/SITE/data/html_dir/2002/04/19/200204190053.asp, as of June 2002.

Nakagawa, Ryoichi, "Promoting E-Government in Japan," available at unpan1.un.org/intradoc/groups/public/documents/apcity/unpan003812.pdf as of September 2002.

Nash, Tony, "Venture Metrics," *Red Herring,* July 2002.

National Office for the Information Economy, Online Council, Joint Media Statement, March 2002, available at www.noie.gov.au/publications/media_releases/2002/Mar2002/online_council.htm, as of June 2002.

"No Laughing Matter," *The Economist*, May 26, 2001.

"North Korea Online This Year," *The Korea Times*, February 15, 2001.

NTT Corp. annual financial statements filed with the Tokyo Stock Exchange, 2001, 2001, and 2002.

NTT Docomo annual financial statements filed with the Tokyo Stock Exchange, 2001, 2001, and 2002.

Nye, Jr., Joseph S., "Information Technology and Democratic Governance," in Elaine Kamarak and Joseph S. Nye, Jr., eds, *Democracy.com: Governance in a Networked World*, Hollis Publishing, New Hampshire, 1999.

Oehlers, Alfred L., "The Internet and Political Change:  Some Thoughts on Singapore," presented at *Internet Political Economy Forum*, "Internet and Development in Asia," Singapore, September 14–15, 2001.

Overholt, William, "Japan's Economy, at War with Itself," *Foreign Affairs*, January/February 2002.

Pabico, Alecks P., "e-lections Philippine Style," *I-mag*, Vol. 7, No. 2, April-June 2001, available at www.pcij.org/imag/online/e-lections.html, as of June 2002.

Pabico, Alecks P., "Hypertext Revolution:  Text Messaging and the Internet Are Now the Tools of Protest," *I-mag*, Vol. 6, No. 4, October–December 2000, available at www.pcij.org/imag/online/hypertext.html, as of June 2002.

Pao, William C., "Hardware Peripheral Devices To Drive IT Industry: MIC's Tsan," *The China Post*, April 30, 2002.

Park, Jhungsoo, "An Innovative Measure to Anti-Corruption of Seoul: Open System," presentation, available at unpan1.un.org/intradoc/groups/public/documents/apcity/unpan003377.pdf as of September 2002.

Purbo, Onno W., "An Experience in Empowering a Bottom Up Indonesian Internet Infrastructure," presented at conference, "Mediating Human Rights," Curtin University, Australia, February 2002.

Qiu, Jack Linchuan, "Virtual Censorship in China," *International Journal of Communications Law and Policy*, Issue 4, Winter 1999/2000.

Quah, Ernie, and Cheng Hai, "Rapid Deployment of the Internet by the Singapore Government," www.isoc.org, 2002, available at unpan1.un.org/intradoc/groups/public/documents/apcity/unpan004073.pdf as of September 2002.

"Reach China's Politicians via SMS," Reuters, March 6, 2002, available at zdnet.com.com/2100-1105-853389.html, as of March 2002.

"Regional Economic Survey: Silicon Valley," *Red Herring*, July 2002.

Satyanarayana, J., "Challenges of E-Government: Two Success Stories from India," 2002, available at unpan1.un.org/intradoc/groups/public/documents/apcity/unpan003379.pdf as of September 2002.

Sen, Krishna, and David Hill, *Media, Culture and Politics in Indonesia*, Melbourne, Australia: Oxford University Press, 2000, p. 194.

Struck, Doug, "Internet Changed Culture of S. Korean Vote; Citizens Web Page's Role in Exposing Candidates' Pasts Exemplifies Political Tool of the Future," *Washington Post*, April 15, 2000.

Taiwan Market Intelligence Center press releases, various dates, available at mic.iii.org.tw/english/ as of March 2003.

Taiwan Semiconductor Manufacturing Corp. annual financial statement, 2001, filed with the U.S. Securities Exchange Commission.

Takada, Aya, "Worry Over GMO Food Slowly Growing in Japan," *Reuters World Report*, October 28, 1999, available at www.seikatsuclub.org as of June 2002.

*Thai Economic Monitor*, July 2001.

Tom.com quarterly financial statements filed with the Hong Kong Growth Enterprise Market Securities and Futures Commission.

United Nations, Division for Public Economics and Public Administration, *Benchmarking E-government: A Global Perspective*, 2002, available at www.unpan.org/dpepa.asp as of September 2002.

"Vice-President, former President Attend pro-Taiwan Internet Radio Launch," *Taipei Times,* May 13, 2002.

"Vietnam to Crack Down on Net Access," *The Guardian,* August 16, 2002, available at www.guardian.co.uk/internetnews/story/0.7369,775745,00.html, as of September 2002.

Wescott, Clay G., "E-Government in the Asia-Pacific Region," 2001, p. 3, available at www.adb.org/Documents/Papers/E_Government/egovernment.pdf as of March 2003.

Williamson, Hugh, "Survey-Asian ITC," *The Financial Times,* December 6, 2001, p. 4.

Wong, Loong, "The Internet and Social Change in Asia," *Peer Review,* Vol. 13, No. 3, 2001, p. 385.

World Bank, *World Development Indicators 2000,* Washington, D.C., 2001.

World Bank case study, "Gyandoot: Community-Owned Rural Internet Kiosks," available at www1.worldbank.org/publicsector/egov/gyandootcs.htm, as of August 2002a.

World Bank case study, "Land/Property Registration in Andhra Pradesh," available at www1.worldbank.org/publicsector/egov/cardcs.htm, as of August 2002b.

World Bank case study, "OPEN: Seoul's Anticorruption Project," www.worldbank.org/publicsector/egov/seoulcs.htm, as of August 2002c.

World Markets Research Centre, "Global E-Government Survey, 2001," available at www.worldmarketsanalysis.com as of September 2002.

Wu, Sofia, "Mofa to Launch Internet Letter Campaign for Taiwan's WHO Bid," *Central News Agency,* May 2, 2002.

Yahoo! first-quarter 2002 financial report (10-K form), filed with the U.S. Securities Exchange Commission.

Yamazaki, Atsuhiro, "Mahathir To Bow Out Amid Drama," *Nikkei Weekly,* July 1, 2002.

Yan, Junqi, "Going All Out to Forge Shanhai's E-Government in the Information Economy Times," at the Third Forum on City Informatization in the Asia Pacific Region, available at unpan1. un.org/intradoc/groups/public/documents/apcity/unpan004298. pdf, as of August 2002.

Yu, Verna, "Hong Kong Gets Smart ID," *The Australian*, March 19, 2002.

Yu, Chi-chang, and Robin Chang, *Developing Strengths of Small and Medium Enterprises in Taiwan*, Lee and Li Attorneys, May 4, 2001.

Zhang, Junhua, "Will the Government 'Serve the People'?" *New Media and Society*, Vol. 4, No. 2, 2002, p. 163.

Zhang, Junhua, and Martin Woesler, eds, *China's Digital Dream*, Germany: University Press Bochum, 2002.

Zunes, Stephen, "Non-Violent Action and Human Rights," *The American Political Science Association Online News*, June 2000, available at www.apsanet.org/PS/june00/zunes.cfm as of June 2002.